ALSO BY DAVID THOMSON

Try to Tell the Story

Try to Tell the Story

A MEMOIR BY

David Thomson

Alfred A. Knopf   New York   2009

THIS IS A BORZOI BOOK
PUBLISHED BY ALFRED A. KNOPF

www.aaknopf.com

Library of Congress Cataloging-in-Publication Data
Thomson, David, [date]
Try to tell the story : a memoir / by David Thomson.—1st ed.
p. cm.
ISBN 978-0-375-41213-4
1. Thomson, David, [date]—Childhood and youth. 2. Film
critics—United States—Biography. 3. World War,
1939–1945—Children—Great Britain—Biography.
4. World War, 1939–1945—Personal narratives, English.
5. Fathers and sons. I. Title.
PN1998.3.T469A3 2009
791.43092—dc22
[B] 2008019605

Manufactured in the United States of America
First Edition

For Michael Ondaatje

FIRST PART

I

MY GRANDMOTHER TOLD ME one morning that Hitler might be hiding on Tooting Bec Common. "Adolf Hitler," she added. I was four, but it was the spring of 1945 and boys knew who Hitler was. Nearly every day in the papers there was a picture of him, the unsmiling pale face stamped on the page, the mustache like a scar. He was missing. He might be dead—shot, burned, poisoned, whatever anyone could think of. But we did not know that then. There was no official report. He might have been taken by the Russians, for sport or research. And so the word had spread that he might have slipped through the closing trap in Berlin. Such magic would make it more plausible that he was the Devil. And there were hiding places on Tooting Bec Common, the surprising extent of open land that began at the end of our road. The Common was my playground, and I knew dells and glades where the desperate might hide.

I say the word had spread, and my grandmother had

her way of suggesting that she led a rich and full life, with many chatting acquaintances. But I never saw them, and never really read any message save for her solitude, her loneliness. I should have guessed that she had made it up. She made everything up, including her own superiority in life—and that can prove an odd training for a grandson. But it was tough enough to regard it as my duty, to go out there on the Common, beating the bushes for the sleeping Adolf. Wouldn't he have Alsatians sitting at his side, too grave to wake him, but so alert as to seize me silently? I knew the Alsatian was a German dog. I wondered why Grannie didn't speak to people and have Hitler dealt with. She read my thoughts.

"Of course," she said, "the glory could be all yours."

You may begin to appreciate my perilous state—that, still only four, I was reckoned to be susceptible to "glory." But the word and its power had reached into me already, and I think Grannie had put it in, like the doctor with the wooden spatula looking for bad tonsils. "Glory" shone from the newspaper pictures of the Victory parade in London later that summer. It must have been a Saturday march, for the Sunday papers were full of it, and we took half a dozen Sunday papers (instead of any church attendance). Representative troops of the Empire had come to London: the Aussies in their slouch hats, Indians in turbans, Greeks in dresses, and the Gurkhas, little fellows with moon faces and what Grannie called "wicked knives." We cut out pictures of these florid regiments for a scrapbook, and there was Grannie, supervising the work, saying "Glorious" under her sour breath. It was as if the war had been fought to rescue her. And it was glorious, too, when she had taken me out to a street corner not far from where we lived, and she had ordered the gathering crowd aside with, "Let the boy see Winnie!"

So I had been sucked to the front and I had seen him, the Prime Minister, sitting in an open car, Winnie, Churchill, a pink face in a black suit—and I was pretty sure that he had seen me, picked me out, and given me not just his "V" signal but a special grin of encouragement. And when I was restored to Grannie, she had whispered, "Glorious." I felt sure she must know Winnie personally— and I did wonder, if Hitler was on the Common, whether it wasn't really more up to Churchill to find him than to me. Presumably he had bulldogs ready to stare those Alsatians into whimpering Nazi dismay.

There was "glory" too in a blue-bound book that sat on Grannie's shelf. It was a famous book, as it happened, the journals of Captain Robert Falcon Scott on his disastrous expedition to the South Pole that ended in 1912. Grannie read to me from the book in her clear, piercing voice— about the hard sledging, the cold days when motors, ponies, and dogs all having failed, Scott and his last few men had begun to pull the sledges themselves. Grannie did not read the end of the story to me. I think it was regarded as something I could not bear. But Scott's bleak words and her tragic delivery left me in little doubt. It was a disaster. Albeit one couched in "glory."

I played the Scott game. I took the clotheshorse and draped it with a blanket. That was my tent. I had a cushion for a sleeping bag. And then, with iron rations—a digestive biscuit, most likely—I lay shivering in my tent, waiting for the blizzard to abate. I was quietly amazed at my courage, and sustained by the "glory" of it all, and Grannie peeped in occasionally to make sure I was not dead yet. She would feel my pulse, with the hand on which she had only three fingers. She had been born with that distinction—I daresay our line was unsound (it helps explain a lot). And I was used to just the three fingers, though I noticed every time that while I was on the brink of South Polar freezing, her hand was far colder than mine.

THIS WAS IN A PLACE called Streatham, SW 16, a bit of London's infinity, in a small section of residential houses named for lakes in the Lake District—so there was Ambleside, Rydal, Riggindale, and Thirlmere, and the last contained our house, number 10, about halfway down the road. Our house was semidetached with number 8, but there were some single houses on Thirlmere and I would guess that when the street was made, early in the twentieth century, it was a well-to-do development. The houses— maybe they were called villas—were built with large rooms and high ceilings on the ground floor and had cellars and attics. There was a manhole for coal delivery in front of the house where I could get in in an emergency, working my way over coal heaps, through the cellar and up to the ground floor.

It was a nice, quiet road. In those days hardly anyone there had a car and the kids learned soccer, playing with a tennis ball on the steeply cambered streets. Each house had a front garden and a back and there were old men—tanned and calm—who worked as gardeners. There was a dairy delivery every day except Sunday—nothing happened on

Sunday then—and a horse-drawn greengrocer's cart came round twice a week. I had the glorious task of shifting the providential manure onto the roses in our front garden. And, as I said, there was the Common at the end of the street. All this and Streatham High Road with its shops within easy walking distance. So it was just bad luck that there had been a war, with the main railway line to the South Coast ports only a few hundred yards away. Diligent Germans aimed at that rail link for years, with the result that our house was hit three times by bombs or bits of their fire. Or so I was told. It was my father's straight-faced humor to suggest that Hitler was targeting me personally because somehow if I survived he knew his Reich was curtains. It was not a joke he was telling. It was a strange, hopeful gesture—a way of saying don't worry if you're unknown. Even the great ones, like Hitler, need to think you might be a hero. A lifetime later, I remember being strangely moved by the story line of the film *The Terminator*, where an agent of the future has come back in time to destroy the seedling of the boy who may make a great rebellion.

I do not really doubt the three blows to the house. After the war, due to the damage, about six feet was chopped off one wing. And the attic was burnt out. I remember the smell as well as the Sunday-afternoon incident when a man on the street waved to my father at an upstairs window. My father opened the window and the man down below said, "Excuse me, sir, but I believe your roof is on fire."

"Good Lord!" said my father. "So it is! Thank you, very much." For it was Sunday and all agencies ran slow on that day. The fire was put out but the attic was useless and it was very hard to get repair workers during the war. So three is plausible.

I was apparently there at the time, but I cannot remember any explosions or fires. I do recall the discovery, on some frosty morning, that the house at the end of the street was no more than a shambles of black, smoking timbers. There were bomb sites all over the neighborhood. Why not us tomorrow?

I do remember lying in the air-raid shelter. It was an iron cage, a rectangle, with sleeping places and survival rations and drinking water, too. The theory was that if the house was hit by a bomb and collapsed then the shelter's structure would stay intact and there would be a chance to dig the survivors out. I lay in that cage, with my mother, and Grannie and Miss Jane Davis, hearing the great sounds in the sky. Perhaps it was German bombing raids, perhaps it was Allied flights going the other way a year or two later. I know now that Streatham—whatever its perils—was a holiday next to Dresden. But Germany had asked for it, hadn't they?

I don't list my father in the air-raid shelter because it was family legend that he didn't use it—not just because he didn't use the house itself that much, but because when he was there and the air-raid siren sounded, he disdained safety or precaution. It was his contribution to wartime morale, I suppose, or some sublime mixture of arrogance and laziness. My mother said it was because he snored so badly—and, alas, as the same affliction has overtaken me, I suspect that may have been the case.

In later years, I recall my mother sometimes being asked whether she thought my father was sleeping with other women.

"Not likely," she said—she had a nice South London voice, proper but a bit sly. "He'd wake up bears in January."

Our house, number 10, was three floors on an open plan. Grannie lived on the ground floor. I lived on the middle floor, with my parents. And Miss Jane Davis lived on the upper floor. That meant that when Miss Davis came home from work, she came in the front door, walked down Grannie's hall, went up one staircase, proceeded through our hall, and took another staircase up to her floor. There was not a lot of privacy. Let me add that there was one bathroom and lavatory in the whole house, on our floor. So all bathroom trips, day or night, involved this small but distinct transgression on someone else's living space. You are wondering whether one bathroom in a house like that was against the law? Or something Hitler had done away with in Germany? I don't know. But there was an extra reason for feeling a little squeezed.

My grandfather—I never knew him—Alexander, he was called, had died in that very bathroom. The hot-water heaters in those days were inclined to give off poisonous fumes. He had fainted and then drowned. That was the story, though my mother could and did hint that maybe Alex just couldn't stand Grannie. (Hitler I know was very bad, but other people—relatives—might be harder to take.) It was my mother who had found him dead in the bath, and I sometimes used to play hell with her nerves when I was soaking in a bath by deliberately not answering when she knocked on the locked door and asked, "Are you all right, love?" That was wicked, but the drama took me.

I mean, "all right" covers a lot of ground, doesn't it? So it takes a pretty stupid man to admit he's all right.

.   .   .

GRANNIE OWNED THE HOUSE—at least I think she
did, though Dad was a natural at taking the onerous cares
of property ownership off your hands. Dad and Mum
moved in sometime after they married in the mid-1930s.
And Miss Jane Davis was the tenant upstairs. I was an only
child. You only a child and an only child? they used to ask,
and it was taken for granted that having no brothers or
sisters put me at a horrible disadvantage. And technically
the answer was no—or yes, depending on the question.

Then there was my uncle Brian, my father's brother. He
was two or three years older than my father, who was born
in 1908. I had seen Brian a few times at our house. He
would come over to visit his mother, though I gathered
that he was not welcome and that my father refused to see
him. He hated his brother and never talked about him. The
remarkable thing about this was not the hostility between
brothers, but the implacable resolve that it exposed in my
father.

To this day, I don't know the details of what had happened with Uncle Brian. I was led to believe that there had
been a matter of fraud, with my father being compelled to
pay back some money for which he had no responsibility
except the need to save a worse fate. I don't see any reason
now to trust what I was told. There were all manner of lies
in the house. My mother said Uncle Brian had been to
prison. I met him a couple of times and he seemed amiable
enough—but I'm sure frauds are like that. It wasn't that I
liked him, but he had three children—my cousins!—named
Terry, Patricia, and Deirdre. I hardly knew them and they

were all maybe ten years older than I was but I liked them in the silly, vague way that assumed they were on my side. Uncle Brian died while I was still in my teens, but the rift was complete and utter. I have not seen those cousins again in fifty years. Even now I wonder if any of them are left alive.

When I was a child, it was the way things were, so I did not question it much. But later on I came to realize how strange it was that a small family had willed itself that much smaller.

But now we come to the big thing—the harder thing to explain. Why did my father, Kenneth, marry my mother, Norah? They were both attractive—my father not very tall, but an athletic powerhouse, dark, boyish, and apparently a source of laughter. He told jokes. My mother was his height, slim, dark, very pretty—I know, that's how I saw it, but there are pictures that back me up. She had a touch of Celia Johnson. They had met at a tennis club. My father was a very good club player and he had rather picked her as a partner. She told me she had loved him at the time, and it is the only possible explanation for a marriage between two people so ill-suited.

My mother had a secretarial job before they married, and she kept it afterwards. She enjoyed the work, but I think her great longing was to have a child. My father did not want children. And a time must have come when he made that clear.

"I tricked him," my mother told me years later. Not that she was a trickster character—not nearly as much as he was. But somehow she must have persuaded him that she was protected, or that the dates were wrong. Or did she get him drunk? Or drive him wild with lust? There is a photograph of my mother in a white nightdress in our back garden. It's a snap taken at night with just the light from the windows picking up her nightdress and her smile. It's inexplicable in terms of the mood of our other photographs. It's like a shot from a movie. Yet someone took that very romantic picture. Someone was there. At night. And I cannot believe that my father had that much longing in him.

At times in my life I played with the notion—the hope—that my father had been someone else. Like Orson Welles or Denis Compton. But this was a tough case to make in that I resembled my father in so many small, irritating ways. So Norah told Kenneth she was pregnant and he said he wasn't having any of it.

"What do you mean?" she asked.

"I'll leave," he said.

She went into the nursing home in Balham in February 1941 to have me. They were living at 10 Thirlmere, and that's where she took me afterwards. But my father was already gone. Just as he had said.

2

I T WAS NOT MY WAR. At its conclusion, I had no
notion of why it was being fought, except in terms of
survival. I could see and count bomb sites on our local
dart board. Soon after the war was over we went to a sea-
side beach, hoping to swim, but as the tide went out it
revealed a litter of concrete blocks, posts, and barbed wire
planted to stop invasion. It was a shocking sign of pleasure
being given up.

Britain had withstood the threat. As I was born in February 1941, the trick of my conception must have occurred
in May 1940, just as the most dangerous time was beginning—what would be called the Battle of Britain, when we
had about half the number of planes available to the
enemy. If the RAF lost control of that summer sky, landing
craft would have been free to come and go. Historians now
say, well, maybe. They surmise that Hitler was cautious,
and too ready to believe that a part of British society was
tempted to welcome German efficiency. Every Briton who

was alive then wonders what would have happened if a German invasion had succeeded. I asked my mother why she wanted a baby at such a time of risk, and she said she had simply wanted a baby. My father's coldness was her Nazism. How do you balance such things? People risked Auschwitz to stay for a kiss. You can say they didn't know what Auschwitz would mean. But they only dreamed what a kiss might bring.

If you look at the history of the war, I think that the British at the time believed the Germans were fierce, thorough, greedy for land and power, humorless, cruel—but no worse. Whatever was known by people forced to flee Europe, or by the British command, I don't think that much was made of the camps, the thought of genocide, the torture and worse. The Germans were greedy bullies and "Mr. Hitler" had bitten off more than he could chew. "Jerry" was a good fighter, make no mistake, and he was led by a madman. But there was not too much wondering about how a madman had taken over a modern nation.

Germany had been presented as insatiable, and out of order. That's what made the war just. So much of Europe had been seized and occupied. That's how Britain could feel relief. Yet this war had been declared over Poland's violation. And in the spring of 1945 Poland was not free, whatever anyone said. That was overlooked, along with the fate of so much of central Europe. Justice had settled for the best deal available, and Germany had been revealed.

As Grannie read to me from the papers that spring, there were pictures I was shown. They were indisputably terrible. As it seemed to me that there were people in loose pyjamas, with eyes too large for their faces, people who had been liberated at one camp or another. These were not the worst pictures. Even in incriminating an enemy, I do not think our newspapers then would have run pictures of the heaped, naked corpses, so slender, so intimate that they were locked in lovemaking positions.

Of course, that is my memory describing them—not me at four and a bit. But there was no escaping the faces of these creatures, or their experience. No one told me they were Jews. I didn't know what a Jew was. No one said the war had been fought to save them, as opposed to saving us. But they were something the Germans had done, or left. And it meant the beginning of an attitude to Germany of which I am not proud. Apart from changing planes in Frankfurt once, I have never been to Germany.

That's not just or sensible. And even if I can trace the great load of anti-German myth dropped on my childhood, it's hardly useful or merited. I have been treated with kindness and respect by modern Germans. I esteem many works and ideas that come from that country. I am as interested in Vienna around 1900 as in any time or place. And history moves on. History is a blink. No matter our outrage at the events of September 11, 2001, we must be ready to be friends and partners with those people who did it.

No one spoke to me about Jews or Jewishness. There were two houses on our street that were lived in by Jews. There were the Schencks, who were Dutch jewelers, with premises in central London. They were smart, quiet, rich, and honored. Then there were the Hilsums, a man and a woman, much poorer and shabbier. They were what was called "rag-and-bone" people. They collected scrap and junk, and then every weekend they went off to a street market, Petticoat Lane, with a sack of things to sell. My father spoke of them as "Jew-boys" and "Yids." They were said to be "dirty," and he asserted that money was their driving instinct. The Schencks, far wealthier, he left alone, except for a "Good morning." I do not mean that my father derided the Hilsums to their face, on the street. He was polite enough in public, but in private he was on the Hilsums always. He was an ordinary anti-Semite, I suppose, and he never referred to the people in pyjamas as being Jewish. The war had been a matter of British survival, and people walked past the matter of the Jews and what happened to them as if on the other side of the street.

The second war had seemed like the first—a continuation of it, even. But I know in 1945, already, I began to see it as the acting out of a new idea, and the idea was Death. It had two great warnings: the people in their pyjamas, and the heat of the sun on the streets of Hiroshima in August 1945. Regular disasters and outrages in war are buried in adjustment and familiarity. But the camps and the Bomb said, See what we can do. They were ominous and they were meant as a message—and they suggested that saying the war was over was hopeful or artificial at best. The war's readiness could continue, and it did. I was moved and daunted by the heights of fear I had missed, like that of Anne Frank hearing footsteps on the stairs. That sort of noise was more frightening than a bomb's blast. Anyway, as wiseacres joked in the days of the V1 and the V2—the flying bombs—"You'll never hear the one that gets you."

I suppose I understood that a great many of "our" soldiers were somewhere away, in another country, fighting and winning the war. In the pages of the *Daily Express* and the *Daily Mail*—before they were twisted for lighting a fire—Grannie and my mother showed me the overall pattern of battle and the black arrow-thrusts pushing into Europe and converging on Berlin. I had an uncle who was somehow involved in this great effort, and there was the father of my best friend, who lived across the street. I had never seen either of them.

Because of some strange privilege my father came home on weekends. It was not known where he was at first, but then the word came that he had taken a job with Philco, an American company that made radios. He was a businessman, a company manager. He never made radios himself. But because the radios were installed in military aircraft, it was reserved work. He was not subject to call-up. That was the story.

Philco was a long way away, somewhere on the far northern side of London. When I was old enough to understand any of this, my mother told me it was too far for a day's journey. And I daresay that was so. London then felt as large as a country. So he came home on weekends, though not every weekend. It was like two weekends in three. If ever I grew old enough to ask where he was, the cause was not his whim, his freedom—whatever he wanted to call it—or his hostility to the idea of a family, but the needs of war.

That was the easier explanation. So many men were away. So many in uniform. And the war's pressure was so extensive that it was easier to think your father had some unusual, or secret, obligation, something not like those other men, something mysterious and confidential. War so often generates social change—and so the failure of our family, or its collapse, was covered up by the dream of military need. I suppose if I'd been a little older I might have been proud of my father, and wondered if he was a spy. He was thirty-three when I was born, very fit, athletic, and smart-looking. There must have been people who looked at him in a suit or a tweed jacket and flannel trousers and wondered what he was really doing.

You see, in most of this, I am reconstructing what I thought of Kenneth Douglas Thomson later—as if he were a strange case or puzzle made for me alone. And that was true, I think—who else cared to explain him? But my main sensation was of his strength and confidence—he must have been holding me—and his tweed, his bristled cheek, and the scent of pipe tobacco—he must have been holding me against him, as close as could be. I felt he was mine and I was his, even if I was blind. But I never heard him say he loved me. In all our time together he never made that incriminating statement.

3

OF COURSE, MY MOTHER, Mum, was there all the time—not to mention Mummy. If I have made less of her so far than Dad or Grannie it is because they were like spectacular visitors, while Mummy was the weather, or the number of steps from my bedroom door to the bathroom so I could count the way in the dark. Grannie had a cold touch and fierce old perfumes, scents that had turned acid over the years. Dad was the pipe and his rough clothes; he was Wills's Cut Golden Bar tobacco. But my mother was scent itself, or breathing. I was breast-fed, I know, and later I asked my mother whether the milk in her breasts was not nervous or afraid sometimes, waiting for the air-raid warning. I wondered whether she had to tell her own milk to be still and calm—I feel something like that sometimes when I write, as if the orderly vision, or its quiet, rhythmic tale, could save me.

I do not recall my mother's smell or feel so much as I do the passage of breathing. I am guessing that she let me fall asleep on her as an infant in the otherwise empty bed. And since that happened—I know it—I am not very interested in whether books on child rearing approve of it. She had not been educated past sixteen. But she knew what she knew, and she knew "common"—common sense. If a thing felt right she trusted it. So she held on to me, I'm sure. My father—coming home now and then, his status so very uncertain—admonished her. It was one of the few conversations she ever reported to me. He said the close physical rearing would soften me, spoil me, and so forth— and so from this distance I spit in his eye as a softie. And I wonder if he grew jealous, or more lonely, in seeing something he had lost. For the coming back did nothing to stop his losing.

The other day—here and now, 2007 in San Francisco— I had a massage. As it neared its end, and the masseuse was working on my head and neck, I had a remarkable sense of my mother's presence. I didn't see her, or smell her. It wasn't that she walked into the room and watched or said anything. It was just that I suddenly felt that the air around me and the hands of the masseuse were my mother's lap. There was no spiritualist affirmation, but I think somehow that Katie, the Californian masseuse, had touched me as my deepest memory recalled. And I was surrounded by my mother—as if I were in her womb still. It's not so odd: if the scent of a madeleine in tea can free so much, then surely a touch—a way of being touched—can restore history and that ancient now.

My mother was a daily routine of which I recall just the big events. Every day we would walk up to Streatham High Road to do the shopping. We had no refrigerator then, so food was purchased nearly every day. I was in my pram and then my pushchair, and I was known on the High Road for having a stub of pipe in my mouth—it was one of my father's pipes, cleaned up for my use, and I think it was judged to be comic or barbarous. But we did the tour of shops and I remember how there was lingering and chatter at the butcher's, my mother laughing at the men's jokes and getting just a little bit over our ration. I daresay many women did that, a touch of flirt for a little lean meat—war makes adventurers of everyone. And while this chat went on I would look into the sides of beef hanging on the walls, many times larger than I was, body caverns with brown meat and yellow fat and flies slow and heavy with their bombs—the beef was hung in the shop during the day. A little touch of the upset—the tummy—was common in those days. We had no Health yet. We took such chances.

And so we came home from the shops. We lunched. We took a walk on the Common—it was so big, it was years before I had the map of it secure in my head. We came home, had high tea, and listened to the radio—to *Children's Hour*, the *News*, and things like *Dick Barton—Special Agent*, before I was ready to sleep. Always the words at the close of day, in a voice like my mother's—that could slip from South London to country. But a nice, soft voice like fur in the dark.

"Are you asleep yet, then?" another voice asked. Who was that? I must have imagined it, a voice in the story, my older sister perhaps?

No, I had no brothers or sisters, but I did talk to my mother about the possibility and sometimes there was a dreamy openness, a wondering in her voice. As if to say, well, maybe there was still a chance. What was she dreaming of for herself—another trick? Another man? But I wanted an older sister—the whole sister feeling was based on someone more knowing than I could ever be. And my mother went through Life Studies in a way that explained how the provision of an older sister now was out of the question. "But people keep imaginary friends," she said—and I knew she must have the habit herself.

"What do you mean?" I asked.

"Well," she said, "someone to talk to. Someone they see. But only them."

It was not so long afterward that my mother and I saw a film called *Harvey*—it is the one in which James Stewart has a friend, a white rabbit, that no one else sees. I was delighted, not just by Stewart and his friend, but at the evidence of my mother being correct (always). And the private pact worked very tidily. No one saw or heard Harvey except the hero. In all the magic of films, this device seemed rather down the list. I loved its ordinariness, and I have always believed that in the dark special effects should be as natural and calm as possible.

"If I had had a sister," I persevered, "what would you have called her?"

"Oh, Sally," my mother said. "If you had been a girl you would have been Sally."

"Sally," I said, and I only repeated it a thousand times.

"That's right, Sally," she said—*she* said it, *Sally* said it—proud of the name but teasing me, too, for having come near it. My mother was sitting on the bed reading to me in just a low lamplight from the bedside table. And there she was—Sally—in the doorway, watching us. A grown-up kid—ten or eleven. She was a silhouette against the light from the hall, and she leaned against the doorpost. She seemed to me very grown-up.

"She's there," I told my mum.

And Mum said, "Oh yes, I bet she is." And then there was just Sally's bells of laughter—butcher laughter, it seemed to me—and I was asleep.

My mother had this fabulous thing, and she gave it to me as a toy.

"You're a liar," said Sally. "You make stuff up."

"I'm not," I said. "I don't."

It was a flying helmet, and it was leather on the outside and fur inside. My mother said it was American. I could put my head inside and inhale the faraway smell of strawberries. I played with it. I don't know how long, a year or a week—and then it had to go back. Sally said so. Not that I ever considered my mother as being under orders, or anything like that. Not that I had any way of knowing how anything as exotic as an American flying helmet could come in and out of our lives. "You think they grow on trees?" asked Sally. She had a kind way of needling me. It was her tone, and one that picked up on the way I would believe anything. I talk to my own children that way. I was her chump, and the charm of it amazed her. I smiled privately, for I loved the way Sally would give me dreamy tongue-lashings. So wicked, so fond and "funny as phone calls." Where did that come from? Had she been seeing pictures already?

But I was amazed and shaken that the helmet—that beautiful thing—had to go away. I nearly lived in it while I could. I wanted to know about the strawberries.

"What strawberries?" said my mum. And she lifted the helmet away from me and sniffed it herself.

"Hair cream, more likely," she said. "I can't catch strawberry." And I never touched it again—out of reach, out of existence, I suppose. Well, what do you think it was all about? There were Americans all over the place— Yanks, they were called—and it stands to reason they noticed anyone as lovely as my mummy.

"Charming!" said Sally.

"What do you mean?"

"I mean, how are you such an idiot?"

"Am not!"

We fought and argued a lot like that, but Mum never came to the rescue or noticed Sally. And Sally, I daresay, wouldn't have been so cheeky if she'd known Mum was listening. But I did ask my mother why a flier—even an American flier—would like to have fur next to his skin.

"Well," she said, "it's like an ice well up in those planes. And fur feels so cosy, doesn't it? So I expect it feels nice if they're afraid."

"Are they afraid?"

"They might be. I would be. Wouldn't you?" Only a woman could refer to this possibility so openly.

I considered the matter gravely. It seemed to me hardly worth having wars if people got afraid. But then my mother was up and into her wardrobe. And from out of the back she found a fox fur. It was a length of fox, with beads for the animal's eyes. And she had worn it once as a young girl, she said. It was mine now, for dressing up. And for some time thereafter I was Foxy the American flier, likely to stun a German with a swinging blow from the head of my fox, and my mum was up for every show.

"You'll go far," said Sally in her knowing way, and she was right. For in a year or two I was wondering whether the great Foxy, our strawberry boy (there wasn't a doubt about it—he had gathered strawberries for someone in that helmet), had been my father or a potential father. I found him a few years later, as Gregory Peck in *Twelve O'Clock High*, and then again years later as Yossarian in *Catch-22*. And when Yossarian is your dream dad, you're in trouble. When I read that book on the London Tube going to work, I had to get off the train because of the feeling of claustrophobia. If the train stopped in a tunnel, and Yossarian was caught in the cockpit with death, I became desperate. This panic came from nowhere. I wouldn't blame Joseph Heller, just his ability to convey the hell of being in an aircraft in 1944. And my life began to change because of not being able to breathe.

"Oh, it makes a difference," said Sally.

4

HERE IS A REAL WAR STORY, and one that tells you about my mother. According to the history books, it was in the summer of 1944 that the V2 bombs began to come. The V2 was a German flying bomb, and it was set to fly for a certain distance. You could hear its drone in the sky. Then the drone cut out. That meant that the rocket and its bomb were falling. That's why you never heard the explosion that got you. It was German and cunning, and altogether nasty. People called them "doodlebugs," and they seemed to come whenever some Jerry had the whim to press a button.

Well, the V2 was the one thing that gave my mother second thoughts about staying in Streatham.

From early on in the war, there had been talk of "evacuating" children to safer parts of the countryside. And it happened—though not to us. Inasmuch as my mother had herself been left by her husband (to look after his son and his mother), I think she was reluctant to quit 10 Thirlmere Road.

But the V2s did make her wonder. I don't know how it happened. I think the mother of my friend across the street heard of a farm we could all go to. It was a farm in Nottinghamshire, and the mother of my friend, Connie—Auntie Connie, I called her—was very encouraging about it. "That's where Robin Hood was from," she said. Well, we got on the train and went.

It was summer and it was a farm with woods and meadows if not quite Sherwood Forest. I know this from a snapshot of me and my friend—Bryan—mounted on a big farm horse, a punch horse. The farmer is standing nearby as if to diminish our evident fear of falling off. And there are many trees in the background.

Somehow or other, we were staying with this farmer and his family. I can remember nothing about them or the place. Apart from the sense of many bad-tempered animals, all of whom we were encouraged to be friends with. I preferred to pursue my imaginary friendship with Sally, because the imagined already meant far more to me than to many people. But Sally had refused to make the trip. She got left behind, along with Grannie and Miss Jane Davis, though I cannot recall Sally ever being in the same space or scenario as those two. Sally already gave intimations of some kind of nightlife in the city. Her age fluctuated. She could be only a year or two older than me, and then she could be a real teenager, with a tongue and a mind of her own.

We had large lavish breakfasts at the farm—many eggs, or far more eggs than we were used to. We got duck eggs, too, all in blue-green shells. This meant being brave enough to enter the chicken "run" or "hutch," a place of dire smells, angry beaks, and a beady eye set on white shins. If you think about it—and I did—a chicken and an egg are implausibly related. It is a good place to start on the incongruities of life: compare the hostility in the face of a chicken with the smooth bounty in a spoonful of fresh scrambled egg.

I don't know how long we were at the farm in Nottinghamshire. It was not too long, but it was long enough for me to observe the bath night of a son of the house who worked at a nearby coal mine. He didn't bathe every day, but on whatever day it was he carried a large tank into the kitchen area where his mother heated saucepans of water to be poured over his grimy body. He sat there in his underpants! It was the bathing arrangement in the household—and my mother, as you may recall, had had ill luck with baths already.

One afternoon, she took me on a country-lane walk. For all I knew then, she was in trembling doubts, wondering whether or not to submit to her own first kitchen bath!

"So how do you like it here?" she asked me.

"I hate it," I said.

She seemed to brighten. "Really? Fresh air, though."

I had never noticed anything wrong with London's air, an observation that reveals my innocence more fully than anything I have said yet. There were strategists of the war who believed that Germany could win just by shaking enough soot and toxic carbons free from existing building structures.

"What don't you like?" she asked me.

In such moments, perhaps, the critical spirit is born. "Everything" would not do, and I probably detected something in my mother that was ready to be talked back onto the London train. Did I know my mother yet? "The privy thing," I said. I hardly knew what to call it. But this bounteous farm, so English in so many ways, lacked a lavatory or modern plumbing. At the end of the garden—ruining the garden's potential as such—there was a shed, a seat, and piles of old newspaper. And a hole in the ground. One seat for the crowded house. One lightbulb. And the full stink of purpose. At my tender age, I had no squeamishness about being or acting spoiled. "The privy is awful," I said.

"I should say so," said my mother, and she looked a couple of years younger on the spot. "You know what? Even if one of Mr. Hitler's specials came through the window, I'd rather be sitting on a nice lavatory than in that privy. This war is being fought for civilization, and if a proper bathroom doesn't count as part of that, then I don't know what does."

I was ready to cheer, and though the sentiment never penetrated one of Mr. Churchill's speeches where Britain would be fought for on the beaches and in the streets, some passing remark on holding Jerry at the bathroom door could not have gone amiss. I was further confirmed in this opinion when my father told me—and where he got this information I cannot imagine—that when the wild Russian cossacks of the steppes rode into Vienna and such sites of sophistication, they were soon seen on the streets sporting the first fruit of plunder—a lavatory seat worn as a collar.

And so we made our way back to that depraved London, where people gambled with bombs for a last few moments of scented comfort. Not that the bathroom at number 10 was ours alone, or anything like it. You remem-

ber that at least five people shared it, though my mother
bowed to no one in the room's décor, its soaps and towels.
It stayed a very pretty room (in gray and lilac), with a carpet over the linoleum and a sturdy air of privacy. The flying bombs were still falling, and my mother allowed how
she was reluctant to get her ticket punched near the end of
the war—as victory seemed more certain. She said it was a
little more scary every day. It was odd: she was eager to
shelter me as much as possible, but sometimes we were
muttering together like two old gamblers hooked into the
green baize. I didn't realize it until later, but her father,
Bert, always played the horses. And my mother (Bert
always called her "Non") loved the word and the idea of
"a flutter," even though she was steadiness itself.

So we weren't quite heroes, Mum and me, even if we
did come back from Nottinghamshire like that. Still, I have
thought about it a lot since and I daresay the people whose
business is going to war should remember that liberty and
so on will go just so far. But if you show people a nice bathroom, they might fight to the end.

When we got back, taking the bus from the railway station and then carrying our suitcases down the road, there
was Sally sitting on the doorstep in the long summer
evening, getting herself a tan. She was not in the least surprised, or sympathetic. I mean, we had gone away at a time
when no one we knew had a telephone. She might never
have heard from us again. My dad had an uncle who had
gone off, long ago, to Canada. Just sent a letter when he
got there. Prince Rupert in Canada.

"Well, look what the cat dragged in," said Sally to me.
(Actually, the cat—Mackie—was curled up on the step

beside her. And all he brought in during the war was a dead rat every morning. Mackie had his wounds—bits taken out of him—but he was our ace, undefeated, and very smug when sleeping.)

"Hallo, Sally," I said. "It was awful."

"Was it? Well, you want to be more careful on giving up on your old Sal, don't you?" I realized she was the first woman I had left, and I was in tears there on the street in the lovely warm evening.

"Oh, don't cry, love," said my mum, and for days she was telling everyone what a good little boy I had been, hardly ever going to that horrid bathroom and then breaking into tears when I got home. And that sarcy sour smile never left Sally's face. But when she caught my eye, and the praise was pouring down, she'd stick out her wet tongue at me. And then she'd cuff me lightly on the head as she and her jasmine scent passed by.

5

DURING THE WAR people were steadily unwell in ways that made illness seem the norm. Or which left health a mystery. And although I could not realize it at the time, we were deprived of certain foods because of the war. For instance, my mother's mother—Grandma—gave me comic books every week. One of which was called *Film Fun*, which she would read to me. It was all in black-and-white, and it had stories in cartoon form on people like Laurel and Hardy, Abbott and Costello, Joe E. Brown and George Formby. Formby was English—north country—but most of the comics were American and they were always slipping on banana skins.

"What's that?" I wanted to know as Joe E. Brown took another skid.

"That's a banana," said Grandma. And then she cried out to a world at war, "Heavens, he doesn't know what a banana is!" A banana, she began . . . well, it's yellow with a skin that you peel. "And inside there's a sweet fruit. I used to slice it up in banana custard. You'd love it."

"Well, what happened to it?" I asked.

"You may well ask," she said. "The ships that carried bananas are now carrying guns and helmets and tins of Spam. The banana, you see, grows in tropic parts."

"Perhaps," I said—and I considered this a very practical, sensible, and even grown-up interpretation—"the banana has been stopped so that people won't fall over on the skins and hurt themselves."

"What?" she said, and then burst out in laughter. It was the beginning of my reputation as a solemn humorist. "Did you hear what the boy said, Non?" This of my mother, who was making our lunch. It must have been a Friday, the day Grandma got on the 115 bus in Hackbridge and came over to see us. Sometimes the day changed, and—if you can believe this—since she couldn't phone us, because we had no phones, Grandma would post a letter, first post, saying, "I'm coming Thursday instead of Friday," and we'd have the letter by eleven o'clock, second delivery. We were technologically nothing, but the post came three times a day—as if people needed it.

But, going back to the banana, it wasn't such a silly idea if the skin was as dangerous as *Film Fun* said—I could imagine Winnie coming up with such a precautionary measure. Because Grandma had her bad leg and she smoked all the time. Even when reading *Film Fun* she liked to keep a cigarette in her mouth and the smoke went up and hit her head. Without a word of a lie, in her silver-white hair—the kind that red turns to—just to one side of the center was a nicotine flair. Smoked all the time and coughed and outlived her daughter, Norah, Non, my mother. Strong as could be. But always complaining about her leg and her back—indeed, I can still see it now, even as an old lady she used to sit with her legs tucked up under her on her chair. Like a girl. To stop them aching. Sally had the same habit, because she just longed to have Grandma's love. But Grandma never noticed her.

We used to say that Grandma and Bert lived in Mitcham, to the south of Streatham. But it wasn't really Mitcham, not in the way Mitcham was Fair Green, the pond, and the cricket green. It was past that, over the Common, past the Mitcham Junction station. Beyond an army camp, and out into flat fields where cows fed and you could see all the way to the great cooling towers in Croydon. It was like country there, in a little stretch of houses called Hackbridge. And it was there my mother's family had always lived.

We had a Christmas there, and it was a bad winter so I think we had to stay longer because of the snows. Grandma washed clothes in a big saucepan (she used the same one to steam Christmas puddings), and then they were wrung out in a wringer. That contraption fascinated me, and one day as I saw the moisture squeezed out of the clothes I stuck in a finger to see what would happen. That finger—the middle one on my left hand—still has the scars on the end section. I cannot recall the pain or the treatment, yet I feel Bert's arm around me as a kind of silent solace.

Bert was the head of the family—he was Grandpa, really, but he wanted me to call him Bert. He was a sweet man, well read, a clerk in the City of London. He had a bad arm—I don't know how he got it—and he couldn't lift it, or tie his tie. But with just one arm at Christmas he had the knack of diverting my attention and slipping silver threepenny bits, as thin as petals, into my Christmas pudding, and then once, for the Queen's coronation, a sovereign. And he had a terrible cough for years before he got ill. He had a lovely smile, naughty, I suppose—and I did hear later that as a semi-invalid he had been a shy ladies' man. He was very polite to women, and there were some men who couldn't talk to women without mocking them or tearing them off a strip. Where did that come from?

Bert had books, a modest library, and he had a practice on weekends of taking a train and walking out to a nice country pub. Sometimes my dad and I would go with him, and Bert was very good on the trees and the birds in the Surrey hills. He loved Box Hill and Leith Hill, Dorking, Abinger Hammer, and the Spectacle Woods in Ranmore— places like that. He seemed like a country person to me, and his love of horses was a part of that character. After all, you could hardly have a horse in Streatham—though people did ride on the cinder track on the Common. He went to the races on Saturday afternoons, Sandown, Kempton, Hurst Park, Goodwood, and Epsom, of course, for the Derby. In the family, it was alleged that he was a dab hand at picking a winner. He studied form and knew how to look at a horse. And I remember Sundays when there was celebration for some coup on the previous day. I hope it was all real. Grandma was skeptical and aggrieved and sometimes said that Bert was like a child in the dark, just kidding himself that he understood anything.

"Well, Lil," he'd say, "I think I understand you." And

she'd sneer or turn very girlish and tell him to get on with it—whatever it was. They were a warring couple, but my mother told me that that was all down to Grandma's hot temper. "She had such red hair once," she told me, "and you can never trust that." Whereas my mother adored Bert and gave him credit for teaching her how to handle the fiery Grandma. Still, I have to say that Grandma never was angry with me. We were pals. She'd take me to the baker, where we'd buy a split tin out of the oven and play games all the way home about it being too hot to hold. And she'd slice the bread so thin you could see the blade like a shadow. Then she'd make hard-boiled-egg sandwiches, the best I ever had, because the eggs were a gooey stage just short of hard. And she'd boil eggs without a timer—would just watch them bubbling and say, "Don't you think they're ready? You don't want bullets, do you?" And she would peel them under the cold tap, like shucking shrimp—too fast to get burned. I still race her, peeling hot eggs for my children.

Here comes another egg. It is a hot day and my mother and I are at the open window of her bedroom, which she liked to use sometimes as a sitting room. And we are looking down at our garden and the next-door garden. The man next door comes out to tend his chickens: he kept half a dozen or so in a hut. He collects the eggs, and sees us.

"Fancy an egg?" he calls out.

And my mother says, "Oh, yes, please."

Whereupon he takes out of his pocket a white handkerchief. He makes a clever pouch of it and puts the egg in the pouch. Then he hooks the pouch on the end of his clothes prop. Every house then had a line for the washing and a prop—a straight, slender branch—for pushing the line as high and taut as possible. (Clothes props were ideal fighting staffs for Robin Hood and Little John, too, and they usually ended as kindling.)

And that's how he does it. He pushes the prop up to us at the window. My mum leans out and gets the egg, like a princess taking a gift of gold. And I look down at the man's face and it's absolutely clear—because I know the feeling— that he's in love with my mother.

An extra egg could mean a happier evening. We used dried egg, too, and I can recall sticking my finger in and out of that jar. The truth is I had to be educated to appreciate real eggs and I still like an omelette made of dried egg and rolled up as tight as a carpet. But better go hungry than eat whale meat. Near the end of the war, the whale was spoken of as our rescue and reward for having so little old-fashioned beef and lamb. You never know—it could happen again. Emergencies come and go, and it is my estimate that it might be wiser to lose the war than have to eat whale meat. Now I warm to Moby Dick as well as the next man, and I am certainly disposed to see many metaphors swimming with the whale. But whale meat—gray, rubbery, chewy, oily, fishlike—is a hazard. As I recall, England turned on the whale in a week. There may have been whale mountains somewhere rotting in the sun. You could not persuade the British to eat it.

The papers said we had won the war the way they said Arsenal 1, Chelsea 2, but we had food rationing for years—into the 1950s, as I remember. There was even the day when a banana boat docked at last, and the claws of pale yellow fruit became available. The children of Britain started falling all over the place, having been well trained in banana-skin jokes.

There was an extraordinary day when a food parcel arrived from Uncle Sid in Prince Rupert. It had apples with skins so thick and red that the white fruit was stained. There were jars of barley sugar and fruit drops. And there were Canadian cheeses coated in red wax. My father did an act where he hacked the wax away, cut into the cheese, sniffed and licked, and declared that it might be British Columbian soap. The food parcel was astonishing bounty and both generous and thoughtful, but it said little for life in Canada. The only thing I liked were the canned pilchards in a heavy tomato sauce. I straightaway assigned them to Captain Scott's sledging rations.

But the diet was a national worry, apparently. The British, the papers said, were not healthy. My mother was troubled by a kind of eczema—it was a rash with sores that affected her thighs and her arms. She used a foul-smelling ointment on it that killed her sweetness for an hour or two, but no one seemed able to explain what the rash was. Until one day, thinking I might be ready for the news, my grandma said it was probably living with my father.

I could not understand how such a malady had come about, especially when Dad was just about the only healthy person in sight. He was all muscle and sinew. He liked to run upstairs and on the Common, where we had sprinting matches—it was me as McDonald Bailey of Great Britain against all manner of American sprinters. He sparred. He shadowboxed. He was Freddie Mills or Jackie Paterson. And when he came home on Friday nights and I was allowed to stay up to greet him, he invented soccer in the kitchen, where he was Tommy Lawton firing in "raspers" at the end of the kitchen table and I was Frank Swift beating away the ball made of pink and white cloth. He was unstoppable and breathtakingly admirable, but he stammered sometimes if he tried to talk to me. And what he never did was say where he had been or even acknowledge that he had been away.

6

THE WAR ENDED IN EUROPE—that was the moment of Hitler on the Common and the Gurkhas in the Sunday papers. Across the road, my friend Bryan's father—Tommy Hamilton—came home. He proved to be a very mild, amiable man, not especially bitter or darkened from the war. He became the manager of a branch of the Victoria Wine Company, on George Street off Baker Street, and as such he gave me my first job one Christmas helping the regular van driver deliver boxes of liquor to very distinguished West End addresses. Just as his son Bryan was my natural and best friend, so Uncle Tommy became a feature of my life. And once he was back home, he and his wife Connie had two more children, boys, and then, much later, a girl.

My mother had a younger sister, Trilby, who lived in Mitcham with her parents. Trilby! Immediately, you get a feeling for Bert's library and a clerk's fascination with the story of Svengali and Trilby (published by George Du

Maurier in 1894). Trilby was called Trill in the family, and she had served in the women's army, in sympathy with her boy friend, Reg, who had gone to Europe in the army and been captured in Italy. He had been in prison camps and his health had deteriorated, and the first time I met him was during that spring. I was at the top of a flight of stairs and he was on crutches at the foot.

"Hallo," he called up. "I know who you are."

I didn't say anything. His helplessness frightened me. "You'll have to come down here to say 'Hallo,'" he said, and I went down. I had a game of sliding down that staircase on my stomach, and he was unable to climb it. "I saw you when you were very small," he said. "But you wouldn't remember."

"No," I agreed. I had heard stories about the war but this was the real thing, a wreck come home, hardly able to stand. And Reg would work on the railways, but he would have bad health for another forty years or so. It seems funny to say that, but as I said before, there were many people in those days who weren't right or quite well.

And there was my dad, fit as a flea, the life and soul of every gathering he ever agreed to, and home just these odd weekends, but behaving as if his schedule were the height of normality or even duty.

"Isn't the war over?" I asked eventually. It was my way of wondering when he would be home all the time.

He drew in a deep, thoughtful breath—he did that very well. "Not really, old chap," he'd say. "Not by a long shot." There was a war in Asia, too, he explained, and he found maps to make it seem so. I swallowed that until I heard that the Japanese had surrendered too. But Dad's timetable persisted. There he was on Friday nights getting off a 49 bus at the end of the road—in time I would be there to meet him, and he was always on the same bus. He was so reliable, yet so lost. Then we had Saturday morning—shopping and stamps, with sports in the afternoon. Then on Sunday mornings we'd go to Mitcham, to see Grandma and Bert. Back for lunch, and then he'd read the papers in the afternoon and stick his new stamps in the albums. Sunday evening Grannie would come upstairs for a sandwich supper and we'd listen to the radio for the Sunday-night theater serial. Mondays, before seven o'clock—so I often missed him—he was gone.

It was a little like a military program, and I suppose that encouraged the half-thought that Dad was on assignment somehow. And I wondered if the term of duty would soon be over.

"Well, there's the Cold War, isn't there?" he pointed out.

"Cold War?"

"Here's Mr. Churchill in the paper," he'd say. "Going on about the Iron Curtain. You see, the funny thing about the war was that, big as it was, maybe it wasn't the real war. Maybe we should have been fighting the Russians?"

He explained that we had lots of men in uniform still, with armies stationed all over the world. So there was the same old need for radios. "Radios and radar," my dad said judiciously. "They really won the war." And I was left to imagine that he had been the necessary glue in the whole trick.

You see, he understood the war. He could explain the history to you. Once we walked over to Grandma and

Bert's—a three-mile walk—and he gave a brilliant narrative of the whole show. And we were there just as Hitler
went into the bunker. Story-telling is a knack, and he had
it. Whereas Reg and Tommy, who had been there, if you
asked them to talk about it, they waved you aside and
said, "You don't want to hear about that," rather as if
they'd been there, but in a daze. I had heard grown-up
talks where Dad explained the war to them, and they nodded and drank it in—the big picture. And it was part of his
theme that wars one and two had only been preparing the
way for the big thing—the Cold War, where war was never
really declared, and never settled. No need—it was the natural state of things. And then he'd give me a big smile and
tap me on the shoulder as if to say everything was going to
be all right. He looked happy, and I began to get the idea
that perhaps some people liked war because it kept dull,
ordinary life at bay. And I am not sure, still, that ever since
1939 we haven't had war, a knowledge that everything
could be over before we heard the bang—so why count on,
or be accountable to, anything as stupid as ordinary life?

Was that what it was all about? The fear of being ordinary? And was that what Dad and I had in common
beyond the same know-all attitudes and the moment when
our faces twisted in stammering?

I grew into a terrible anger over it, so that I sometimes
wonder whether all my capacity for anger was drawn off
into that feeling about my father and his lies. Because, you
see, it went on—Jesus, it went on, in its crazy way, until my
mother died in 1976. So you could be furious or amazed,
and long before the end you could see that my father was
nearly mad living that way. He had a terrific air about

being the best-informed and most far-seeing person in the family—really, we were lucky to have him, poor souls— but it left him looking deranged. If you're that smart, we said with wicked giggles, how did you end up with us? Except that, obviously, he did have his other life.

I knew he left at about a quarter to seven on Monday mornings and sometimes I was sorry to see him go because he played with me and took me to sports and told me things like the history of the war. And I still think about those things. But I was "at home," and I had a mum who would look after me. I trusted that. I had seen the checks he left her in his neat hand-writing, which worked out to about ten pounds a week by the mid-1950s. Her money, for looking after us.

But think of it from his point of view. In the dark of the early morning, he has to get away to catch the bus to be back at work—by nine, let's say—carrying his small suit-case like a commercial traveler. And then after a Monday at work, he goes back—where? He told me he had a room in a boarding house but he never gave me the address or a phone number. Suppose it was more. Suppose he had another home—and even another woman? And this started in 1941, or soon after, and don't forget that it went on until 1976. Of course, there was another woman. And all she did was cling to this man who went away every two weekends out of three, and at Christmas, Easter, Whitsun, and August Bank Holiday, and on a "family" holiday with his wife and son, though only for the first week of the two.

7

ON AND OFF DURING the 1920s and '30s, Grannie (her given name was Violet Edith Wharton) and her husband (Alexander, dead in the bath) had had a theatrical company. I'm not sure of its status. But, maybe for charity or hospitals, they went around and put on plays. This was in South London and Surrey, because the family lived in Sutton then. Grannie was the star actress, and though she had—I thought—an unkind, hard face, she had a great voice with unusual carrying power and perfect diction. In our three-storey house, she could talk to you from the ground floor to the top without raising her voice. And Dad had played cameo parts— villains and comics—and I think he had been very happy doing so. He preferred supporting actors at the movies and was reliable for his "turn," no matter that he got no direction or attention. He believed Peter Lorre was a great personality—and so do I, still do. But hardly Dad material.

When Mum got enlisted as Dad's girl friend, she played

a few small parts, but she admitted that she had been nervous and shy. She also told me, in a matter-of-fact way,
that Dad was actually quite good—that you saw something of him onstage (a kind of fun) that was not always
there in life. And I could see that in pretending he flow-
ered, like the hyacinth bulbs we kept in the dark. He liked
to make people laugh: I know it because I have the same
weakness, or the same shy habit of telling stories.

Here's one of his jokes, to give you an idea. He often
had jokes to tell, and they were usually quite long and grew
longer with every telling. This is a joke from soon after the
end of the war, and I'll try to do it in his voice, or his way.

"Did you hear about the King and Uncle Joe?" he'd
ask me.

"No," I said. I had great childish respect for the King,
George VI, and I knew that Uncle Joe was Josef Stalin,
supreme commander of all the Soviet Union and another
big mustache in the papers.

"Well, the King thought he'd try and help with the Russian problem, so he sends Uncle Joe a letter and says, 'Why
not come on a state visit?' And Uncle Joe decides that it's a
good idea. And he comes to Britain, and the King and the
Queen greet him at the railway station and Joe says,
'Where am I staying?' and the King says, 'Ah, well, I've got
you the best suite at Claridge's. It's just up the road from
the Palace. I think you'll be very comfortable.'

"But Joe says, 'I want to stay in the Palace. Buckingham
Palace. With you.'

"The King sighs and says, 'Well, Joe, to be honest with
you, the palace is on the chilly side. We had some bomb
damage, you know, and we can't get the builders over.'

"Uncle Joe sulks and says, 'Palace, or I go home.'

"Well, the King does what he can. He gets the Queen to hurry back home and find the best guest room, and they patch the broken windows. To make a long story short, Joe stays at the palace and he seems to enjoy it.

"So the King says, 'Joe, the Royal Tournament is on—big military show—and I thought you might like to see it.'

"Joe's mouth droops. 'Vould like to see grand assembly of British fleet—at Scapa Flow,' he says.

"This is a tall order. The British fleet isn't what it used to be, and the ships are scattered all over the place. The King tries to explain this and Uncle Joe says, 'You are the King—you fix it.' And the King does his best at short notice. They can't go to Scapa, but the King gets twenty or so ships to Spithead—and Joe seems very pleased. 'Good fleet!' he says. 'Good show!'

"The King relaxes, and he tells Joe about a big treat. They're going to see Laurence Olivier and Vivien Leigh do *Macbeth*—a command performance—the full flower of the English theater.

"Joe frowns. 'Hmm,' he says. 'I prefer *Hamlet*.'

"'But they're not doing *Hamlet* at the moment, Joe,' says the King. '*Macbeth* is the play they've learned. And, anyway, *Hamlet* is long, you know.'

"'I hear *Hamlet* is the greatest play,' says Joe. 'You're the King . . .' Et cetera.

"Olivier has a fit, but he agrees to do it—*Hamlet*, the works. Uncle Joe falls asleep, but he wakes up clapping and pronounces it very good.

"So far, so good. Well, Saturday's coming up, football day, and the King says, 'I thought we might see a match.

And it happens that Chelsea are at home to Manchester United. Should be a cracker.'

"'Arsenal,' says Stalin. 'I like the name Arsenal.'

"'Very good team, too,' says the King. 'But they're playing away this Saturday at Newcastle. Too far to go.'

"And Joe looks at the King and says, 'You are the King—have the game played here, in London.'

"Whereupon, King George VI, bless him—because he never wanted to be King and wouldn't have been but for Edward VIII and Mrs. Simpson, and it was hell on his stammer—says, 'Look, Joe, I've done a lot for you, and I'm happy to do it—but I'm not going to let you spoil my Three Away Winners on the pools.'"

While British readers are rolling on the floor in what used to be called "mirth," I will explain to others that every week in Britain there was heavy gambling—especially among the working classes—on the football pools. The punter had to forecast results. The biggest prize was for predicting eight draws. But obviously the King (a humble man) favored the Three Away Wins pick.

As you can guess, this story could be enlarged with many other steps, even to the point of Uncle Joe demanding a sunny day at Wimbledon. When I was a child, it seemed to me that my dad was a fabulous teller of such stories, and I know when I first heard this one I took it for granted that his special war "service," the being away, had brought him into direct contact with both the King and Stalin. There's something about this story—and its hangdog intimacy—that gets at the "private" life of harassed monarchy, a theme that goes from Charles Laughton in *The Private Life of Henry VIII* all the way to Helen Mirren in *The Queen*. What is the royal family for? So that shaggy-dog stories may be told about their absurd status. What does that do? It makes them human and trivial. With what result? We knock along with them. Yet somehow the silliness of royalty excuses us from final realities—we can't cut off their heads again because . . . well, they'd be offended, wouldn't they. The way they are if you talk to them first. It's a fatuous rigmarole, but it helps explain why an allegedly grown-up nation still drags along with these poor idiots.

But my Dad showed this mystery in himself with the story. In life, he said nothing about himself or his life or what he felt. But in the story-telling, he became large, full of nuances, nooks, and crannies. His King was someone you wanted to put your arm around when words of consolation were beyond the point—and not allowed, because you are not supposed to address the King and Queen until you're spoken to first. Of course, even then there were hints from grown-ups that they'd heard all these stories too many times before. But I was touched and opened up. I'm sure I saw a potential for myself in the expansion of narrative voice—and even a way of seeming frank and honest, while drawing the wool across your eyes.

By which I mean to alert you to the modern disquiet over the "memoir" as a reliable literary form. I am trying to tell you the truth—but I don't think I know the truth. I am still, years after his death, bewildered and pained by my father, and trying to love him—or find his love for me. But he lived in true shadow, and even if he was vivid in telling a story or playing a part, he sometimes left the impression that there was nothing else there. I think I'm reaching out for the idea that, having written a lot about actors, I realize now how far my father raised me to it. And I have very mixed feelings about actors.

But as my father moved so regularly from one household to the other, I wonder how close he came to seeing that lying itself, that becoming a figure in a story but not belonging in life, was his impetus? Whenever I see great pieces of English cross talk—Morecambe and Wise or Harold Pinter—I long for the Pinter play about the state visit of the Russian premier or president or whatever he was and the put-upon King. With my father playing both parts and the farcical melodrama going on forever. Until Uncle Joe says one day, "I vish to see this Kenneth Douglas Thomson . . ." and the forlorn King has to admit, "Sorry, Joe—not possible. He and I have never been caught in the same room together."

Stalin sighs and twists his mustache and is bound to tell the King that this is war, then.

The sad comic was a feature of those postwar years usually on the radio. The fellow would come on, with a whining voice about the glories of peacetime and having won the war, and of course he sounded like someone from a ruined nation. I still don't understand why the British tolerated such a bleak victory for so long, but we did, and the horror of it all was in the melancholy voices of Al Read, Max Wall, Tony Hancock, and even Archie Rice.

The only thing I think I ever heard about my father's other life was years later. I was in my late teens and he was living—I knew from my mother, but not from him—in the St. Albans area. But still he came home. Somehow or other, he learned I was reading Chekhov at school, and out of

nowhere one day he said, "I'm doing Chekhov in a play."
This was a great surprise, not just of having a life filled in
to the least degree but because his manner was not quite
right for Chekhov. Still, he admitted that he was in an amateur theater company, and he was playing one of
Chekhov's old people. He said he found it very empty, and
he was amazed that the play was labeled a comedy when
there were never any laughs. I fear he may have labored to
create them.

"You don't have to laugh out loud at comedy," I said.
Say I was sixteen then, and very snooty.

He looked at me as if he thought—for the first time—
that I might not be his son. And he told another story.

One day, a farmworker was putting manure on a field
of strawberry plants. There was another man watching,
from over the fence of the local lunatic asylum.

"What are you doing, then?" said the watcher.

"Spreading shit on the strawberries," said the laborer
patiently.

"Oh," said the man. There was a pause. "We use cream
here—but, of course, we're daft." Maybe Dad had felt
more in Chekhov than I had.

8

I was very young when I was taken to the pantomime, and I think we went because my father knew people in the show from the old theatrical days. And we sat in the front row of the circle. I can remember holding on to the brass rail on top of the upholstered ledge. Hold on so you don't fall over, I suppose. And the pigeons came and sat on the rail too. Of course, you can do almost anything you like in a pantomime. That's what makes it so rich and interesting. And there must have been a man who did stage magic in which the pigeons flew up to the rail and then flew back on his command. Something like that. And the pigeons came to the rail near me—did Dad arrange for that?—and I cried out "Pidgies!" in my piping voice. I have the vaguest recollection of it—it was always very hard to extricate what had really happened from Dad's account afterwards. Suppose he was telling himself stories all along!

I think the pantomime was *Aladdin.* When it was over

we went backstage to meet the actors. They seemed to be about twenty feet tall, and I was terrified of them, especially the Grand Vizier, who seemed to be Dad's friend. But there were boys in tights and high-heeled shoes who proved to be girls when you got close to them. There was an extraordinary smell, sick but sweet, and I asked what it was. No one knew. No one noticed. Until my mum suddenly said, "He must mean the greasepaint." That was it, and not long after as a kid I was given Leichner makeup sticks, and I had a game of making people up. And I wondered quite early whether, while it was enchanting to see a woman put on makeup—I watched my mum do it very carefully—it was a man's job to put it on for her?

Might have changed the world.

Anyway, I wouldn't talk to the Grand Vizier because he was so huge and villainous. My dad said, "He's scared of everything," and I know I was. But it hurt me that he thought it, and said so. So I clutched the Vizier's outstretched hand, huge and warm and slippery with coffee-colored greasepaint. To think that an actor colored every part of his body with the paint.

"Why do they wear paint?" I asked Mum.

"To shine in the lights," she said.

The Vizier gave me some colored handkerchiefs, which were part of his act. He wore shoes with curled toes and I could not guess how he ever got them on and off. But it was strange that characters who had been enemies in the show were now talking to each other like people standing in the same queue for a bus. While still being as big as the bus.

Not long after that, I was given a toy theater. It was a

cut-out book where you made a proscenium arch and then the box for the stage. There were printed plays with cut-out pictures of characters. They were made by Pollock's—until recently you could still get them at their shop in Covent Garden—and mine was a treasured possession. I needed help with the cutting out, and my mother found tiny lightbulbs and a battery so I could light the stage. I had two plays in the next few years: one was *Treasure Island* and the other was a version of *Hamlet* based on the Olivier film. I experimented endlessly, way beyond those two texts, and I had a story in which Hamlet and his long-lost father, Long John Silver, beat back the world. I noticed that the two plays were alike in that Hamlet and Jim Hawkins had both lost their dads. It worked very well that the cut-out characters were about the same size as my toy soldiers. I saw that the illuminated box was a precious place where any story could be told.

Of course, there was another box, and it was like my theater in that it only worked if a light came on inside. It was the radio—the wireless—though whenever I saw inside there was this jungle of wires, impossible to chart, let alone repair. The radio was large, a piece of furniture, a cabinet with fretwork over the speaker. Hardly anyone then had portable radios, let alone the sort you can pop in your ear. The radio was as immense as a piano, and Grannie had a piano, a baby grand by the French windows. But the piano was out of tune and never repaired, while the radio was alive every evening.

There was much to listen to—there were shows and the news and plays, or books done as narratives. And when I was no more than five, there was a version of *Oliver Twist,* with the noises of the streets and Bill Sikes's dog, and Fagin teaching Oliver how to pick a pocket. We listened to it and then my father replayed the scene, using the Vizier's hand-kerchiefs. His Fagin was probably on the broad side, and so I was not too surprised years later to discover that Alec Guinness's superb Fagin in the David Lean film was regarded in the United States as anti-Semitic.

The idea of following a story like Oliver's week by week was inspiring, though I had no idea then of how far it resembled the pattern of many Dickens publications. I did not understand all of the story, but I grasped the desperate plight of Oliver, torn between vivid scoundrels and insipid goodies who would take care of him. To say that the BBC did such things well is like congratulating Warner Brothers and RKO Radio for capturing a certain mood. And I still believe that radio is a matchless medium, sadly neglected in America, where I live now. This is the story of a lucky boy—lucky to be raised in the age of radio. The BBC—and that's all it was back then—filled the air with plays and dramatizations. They even had a standing company of actors. I thank my stars for Carleton Hobbs, Norman Shel-ley, Grizelda Hervey, Mary Wimbush, and so many others. To this day, though I haven't heard the radio serial *The Archers* for forty years, I know that Ysanne Churchman was Grace Archer and was killed on a shocking night to rival the crash of the Manchester United plane in 1958.

I may not have realized that *Oliver Twist* was Dickens, but the Sunday-night drama was noticed in the house. And thus it was that Miss Jane Davis came to my parents and said . . . Well, what did she say, or how do I put it? Try something like, "Perhapsh de boy shd rrrd a l'lle Dickenge."

This is an inept transliteration, and I have no wish to be cruel. The good news was that Miss Jane Davis was secretary of the Dickens Society. The bad news was that she had an afflicted palate so that hardly anything she said could be understood.

Miss Davis was shy, and the spirit of spinsterhood. But there was no doubt that she was passionately moved by reading Dickens and knowing about him. She showed me her shelves of Dickens books. She made terse, very warm comments about them. She told me how Dickens walked and walked the city to find characters. She had cartoons of Dickens characters—Micawber, Pickwick, Miss Havisham—and she introduced them like companions from life. She urged that I be taken to the 1946 movie of *Great Expectations*, but my mother had heard that the first appearance of Magwitch on the marshes was so terrifying that it was not to be risked. Miss Davis sighed. Yes, it was true, Dickens knew a harsh world of great pain and hardship. But if the boy was in any way attuned to drama, then perhaps the show was more than the terror. Years later, after decades of film study, let alone living in a world of appalling unkindness and cruelty, this still seems to me a besetting suggestion.

I was afraid—for the people in concentration camps, of the Grand Vizier, of my father being away and that my mother, too, might disappear. I was afraid of everything. I still am. But handling fear is a step toward art. And I had heard a bugle call—*Great Expectations*.

"What is *Great Expectations*?" I asked Miss Davis.

"Rrrurding," she said. I couldn't understand. She repeated the word and then opened the book. Her tiny forefinger began to trace the lines of type. I saw how wrinkled it was.

She looked at me. I cannot really remember how she looked. But I recall the weight of her concentration and I think of her now as someone not just proposing Dickens, but emerging from him. "Yes," I said. She died not long after this, and I don't know how. I just saw that she had vanished from the house. She left reading.

SECOND PART

9

"KATE, MY MATE, and I will skate in the park."
This was the opening sentence in my first reading
book at school. There were colored pictures of an
old-fashioned time with children skating, and it looked
like Christmas. But the time was not as old as that of Mr.
Dickens (I had seen the classic illustrations to his stories)
and not as harsh. Kate in the pictures was my idea of a
"silly girl" and, after all, if they were skating, then I
couldn't understand why they were not playing ice hockey.
I don't recall seeing ice in nature that one could trust—or
not until the winter of 1947—but my father had taken me
to Streatham Ice Rink, where there was a hockey team
filled with Yanks and French Canadians who hadn't made
up their minds about going home yet. I loved the way that
without the game being stopped three subs would step
over the wall and glide onto the ice while three others
skated away for a rest. I was mystified by the stupid and
deliberate ways in which the players picked fights—unless

that was what the game was really about. Otherwise, my sporting education was based on being a good sport. Indeed, accepting defeat was what sporting meant, since I wasn't good at games. And I hated it. For I could feel, even if I could not quite see, the absolute need to win.

School provoked a far deeper hatred, a kind of anathema. This had its roots in being separated from my mother and in resisting and dreading the company in and uniformity of school. Though I was responsive to good teachers, I had a deep-seated instinct that education was a private business and responsibility. I had nothing to hate at school. The place my mother chose was near ideal. The people there were tender and smart, and I excelled. I have the recollection that I learned to read my Kate book in a few days. That owed a lot to the letters and soundings I had done with my mother every night, and lying between my mother and father in their bed on Saturday mornings. (Yes, they shared a bed, and yes, they made a nice show of sharing me so that we were a team. To this day, I believe in Saturday as a blessed day and a team day—the holy day in my week because of our threesome as that dawn came in.)

The school was a private preparatory school called Rosemead, and my going there was a sign of my parents' wish for gentility. The fees must have been a test for their odd budget, but the bargain was more than justified. The teaching was expert and careful. The society of little boys and girls was cheerful and enthusiastic. The school uniform was purple. The school's first premises were in Leigham Court Road and then it moved to South Clapham, and in my time there the school was dominated by its owner, Miss Plumridge, a Lady Bracknell figure in my imagination—immense, beyond question, the law, and the way—though I suspect in her own mind she still had a dash of Margaret Lockwood. As a star pupil, I was treated with rare generosity and sympathy, except by a couple of the senior teachers who I sensed had picked me as a self-dramatist early on and were inclined not to be a loyal audience. And I felt I was besieged by girls at the school. All my life, I have practiced keeping team lists. I can reel off the Australian cricket team of 1948—Morris, Barnes, Harvey, Bradman, Hassett, Miller, Tallon, Loxton, Lindwall, Johnston, Toshack—just as I can still give you a list of Rosemead girls I was in love with (for a season or a minute). I fear I was a monster of infidelity: Maureen Bly, Shirley Coles, Lesley Payne, Joan Fletcher, Judith Otter, Susan Frampton. If any of them are alive and reading this I hope they will forgive me for remembering (and naming) them. Not an iota of scandal falls on them, of course. They were real, but they were in my head along with "Kate, my mate," and the voices on the radio, and they were helpless co-conspirators in a dream called romance. At seven or so, I was painfully in earnest about needing to get married. After learning to read, what else was there?

I read anything and everything. I had a very good memory. And I was furiously eager to know about people— what made them function or decide. It wasn't so much an altruistic attention to human nature as a kind of directing instinct: how could you get people to do your will, to be figures in your story or your scheme? It might have looked like kindness—and that may have been why girls were drawn to it—but the impulse was manipulative and creative, not sympathetic. I think I half saw or believed that if you had a place in a story you required no sympathy. Just act your part. It was years before I realized that this mixture of perfection and cold-blooded instruction was vital to the movies.

But I fell ill or faked illness a lot—my father said it was "schoolitis," and he blamed my mother for not seeing through it. So I missed school days that had been paid for, and that sort of deficit always impressed Dad and made him parental. Yet in all my time at school, I never found that I had missed anything important, or anything, at least, that I couldn't catch up on myself. Maybe that is arrogance still, but the confidence grew nonetheless and left me more casual about attending. To this day, I am excited by reports of home schooling or of kids who somehow missed out on "school" altogether, but who turned out to be smarter or more successful than those with formal education. So I love stories about Gore Vidal or Warren Beatty having no college degrees, and I am moved and sustained by the plain evidence that people like Louis Armstrong or Charlie Chaplin survived so many handicaps and deprivations and yet knew the human heart as if they had invented it.

Of course, I cheat: I was sent to good schools, and I was there more often than not on the financial sacrifice of others. I remember the current left by great teachers. So it was my attitude as much as my experience that told me the kid in school was an invader and a pirate—take what you can and trust your own thieving heart. Education rests in your confidence and desire more than in the eventual pouring of 100 cc, or whatever, into your patient glass. So I love stories about people without training or learning who fall into vaunted jobs and carry them off. Impostors can be heroes in my scheme of humbug and hypocrisy. And I have never quite seen that they may be outlaws and murderers in the process. One reason I have aways loved Orson Welles—as a kid determined not to grow up—is that as a child fortune-teller he realized that if you told any suppli-cants that they had a scar on their knee and the shadow of some great sadness, most of them were yours for the rest of the story. Say "Rosebud" with enough religious certainty and you will have most people for a couple of hours. And if you can't put two hours to good effect, then you have no idea of Saturday afternoon and the chance of winning. Orson Welles, you may guess, gave up schooling at sixteen, took a gypsy caravan on a tour of Ireland, and thereafter impressed the many dinner tables of his life as someone who knew everything (including the great difference between the histories and cultural achievements of Switzer-land and Italy as spelled out in *The Third Man*—a primal event in my childhood). That is not education—it is a stage trick, and I fear it may denote the reluctance or even the adolescent refusal to grow up.

"So, who's your girlfriend this week?" It was Sally. I was home from school, unpacking my books. There was a modest amount of homework to be done.

"Oh, I don't know," I said in an airy way.

"I thought I was your girlfriend," she said, and she pre-tended to look hurt.

"You're my sister," I said. "My friend."

"No, I'm not," she said—and I knew she was speaking of danger.

"You are," I said.

"I'm not. Look away and I could be gone. Just like that. Is that what you want?"

"No," I said. "You're not to go."

"Listen to you, giving orders."

"Did you go to school?" I asked her.

"Of course I did. Council school, not like spoiled boys. Bloody hard it was. Lots of fights with other kids. Not your kind of thing."

"But all the things I want to know, you know. I know you do."

"You'd best remember that," she said. "Sally's got her head screwed on."

There was this lovely way in which Sally was always smarter than me, more worldly, no matter she'd missed my kind of school. She said "Rosemead" as if the word were caught in her nose. "Oh, excuse me, *Rosemead*." And she made me laugh and it kept me cheerful. It wasn't for years until I noticed that it was like the way Barbara Stanwyck talks to Fred MacMurray in *Double Indemnity*. But it was too late by then to lose that teasing, alluring voice.

10

H E MUST HAVE MADE the decision, and I am grateful for it. Granted, it was just a few weekends, but my father gave himself to me in the years in which I went from five to eleven. And Mum stood back to let it happen. I have mentioned ice hockey already, but Dad made it his calling to introduce me to any sport being played. Yet I know now that he was already involved with a woman a good deal younger than he was on the other side of London. She was a demanding person, and I suspect that in those first years she might have wanted or reckoned she had a right to children. And whatever Dad had planned when he left us, he was still prepared to give us two weekends in three and to live a life of pretending that he had not really left. I suppose he picked sports as our main shared activity, but he must have seen that I was ready for it. He had been able to play any game he tried and be pretty good at it; more or less, it was the same with me. (Though later, when I went to a posh school—a rugby school—I had to play a game he had never played. So he mocked rugby.)

At some time in the 1930s, he had worked for the management of Wimbledon Stadium. It was not the All England Lawn Tennis Club, but an oval stadium that featured a speedway, dog racing, boxing matches, and various other events. So he knew people in sports, and had a friend, Archie Kempster, who was often offered up as someone who might get us tickets for some big event. It was while at Wimbledon Stadium that Dad—a handy amateur boxer—had sparred with Tom Heeney, the British heavyweight champion who had gone to New York in January 1931 to be knocked out by Max Baer (who later became heavyweight champion of the world). Heeney had liked my dad as a sparring partner because as a lightweight he was quick.

I had a pair of old boxing gloves, and I sparred with my father. He did it to teach me, he said, and I never remember him hurting me. Still, I was the only child I knew who had a subscription to the *Children's Newspaper* and the *Boxing News* at the age of about seven. I read both with total interest, and so it was that I was able to keep up with current fights while enjoying the historical articles about people like Jimmy Wilde, Benny Lynch, Harry Greb, and Stanley Ketchel, "the Michigan Assassin," a man who had given thirty pounds away fighting Jack Johnson.

My father had an old scrapbook with pictures from the fights. There was one of Dempsey hovering over Gene Tunney, refusing to go to his corner. That was the occasion of the long count, when Dempsey threw away the chance to get his title back. There was another of Dempsey being knocked out of the ring by Luis Firpo. But Dempsey, "the Manassa Mauler," got back in the ring and slaughtered Firpo in the next round. There were pictures of the movie-star-handsome Georges Carpentier, and my father told the story of how someone he knew had gone to see Carpentier when he came to London to fight Ted "Kid" Lewis. The man bent down to put his hat under his seat and while he was doing it Carpentier hit Lewis and that was it. First-round knockout. The man never saw a punch.

Boxing was crowded with astonishing stories—the fights between Max Schmeling and Joe Louis, the tragic story of Primo Carnera, "the Ambling Alp." My father said great boxers grow out of terrible poverty, and many go back there afterward. We used to go to the White City to watch athletics, and at the White City station there was always a wreck of a man, sitting in a corner, collapsed and begging, staring through sightless eyes. That's Johnny Summers, my father said, used to be British champion. My father had a lot of boxing talk: the bigger they are, the harder they fall; left hook a southpaw; they never come back; break without a blow. The actor in him liked to give a running commentary on the battle as we were sparring. The contestants were never us; we were Joe Louis and Tommy Farr, Willie Pep and Sandy Saddler, Turpin and Robinson.

In many of the live fights I followed, there was a grim pattern. The British would develop a promising boxer, and he would triumph at home and in Europe. But then he would face American opponents, and it was always the same story. Louis had beaten Farr, the Brown Bomber against the hero from the Welsh mines. Joe Baksi beat

Freddie Mills, Lee Savold beat Bruce Woodcock. It seemed automatic or genetic, and my father said that after 1945 Americans were better fed, which was surely true. But English fighters stood in line to be good, plucky losers against American powerhouses, and it hurt them and me.

Then came Randy Turpin. He was colored (it was plain to see), though he came from the British Midlands. He had a boxing family, and he was West Indian originally. Around 1950, Turpin rose and took the British middleweight title, then the European. He beat everyone he fought. And it was then that Ray Robinson—Sugar Ray— came to Europe on a tour. From May 21, 1951, Robinson had six fights in Europe in five weeks. The culmination was Turpin in London on July 10.

By then, Robinson was weary. He was living well and courting publicity—he came in a pink Cadillac, with a glamorous wife. He likely underestimated Turpin. It was a midweek fight, so Dad was not home. But Mum let me stay up, sitting in bed, to listen to the live radio commentary. It was a close fight, and maybe a British referee favored Turpin. You could say that Turpin was lucky. But after fifteen furious rounds the radio commentator could scarcely believe it himself as the referee went from adding up his scorecard and moved toward the British boxer's corner. I remember the exhilaration in his voice, the disbelief and the relief. "Turpin has won"—and I was standing on the bed using it as a trampoline, being urged to be careful by my mum. The joy was brief but it was intense: Turpin was world champion until September 12, when he went back to New York and Robinson knocked him out. Fair enough, and a proper result, I'm sure, as

Robinson resumed his full professional discipline. Even then, I could sense that Robinson was the more intriguing man—a flashy black showman who talked. He was Ali before Ali. To this day, I want to write a book about the prolonged duel between Robinson and Jake LaMotta (Marty Scorsese's *Raging Bull*), in which Robinson had to beat LaMotta five times in six fights between 1942 and 1951. Think of it, a portrait of America in those giddy but terrible years, with the great duel holding it in place and Robinson as the touchstone of a new country.

My dad never took me to a fight. I asked, and he said, "One day, perhaps." I suspect it was Mum's embargo: it was enough that I knew fighters' records and collected pictures of them. No need to expose me to the real blood, the broken teeth, and the kind of people who ran the fight game. But my father played that side of it for all he could. He said that "Jack"—Jack Solomons, the leading fight promoter in London—had his eye on me as a "crowd-pleaser" and that he was looking for the right fight for me. Jack never materialized (he was from that distant world that had the King and Uncle Joe), but one day Archie Kempster actually appeared, after years of talk and announcement. There he was, in a camel-hair coat and a cigarette holder!

"So what d'you think, Arch?" asked my dad. "Do you think Jack could use this boy?" For a moment they were my Fagin and Bill Sikes, and I have wondered in the years since—what if I had shown real promise at any sport? I didn't, so I was safe. I was competent at some games, but not marked by real class. But if I had, would my father have seized upon it and been my manager, my Jack?

"I daresay he could," said Archie, and I never saw him again. So there it goes, a common regret: I might have been a contender but for my full weight of innocence and maternal protection.

For decades I have had a novel in my head in which a very raw youth has the powers of a chess champion. Sensing money it it, his father takes over the boy's career. His growing up is blocked by hours and years in chess study, until the boy—sixteen or seventeen now—goes away to some remote place for a Masters confrontation. This was based on the Spassky and Bobby Fischer meeting in Reykjavík in 1972. Waiting, waiting for the Fischer character's decision to play, the boy is introduced to life by an Icelandic chamber maid (Charlize Theron with an accent?). He loses the championship but he breaks free from his father and the hopelessly neurotic head he finds on Fischer's shoulders. Is there a Jack yet in publishing who might like that?

II

THERE WAS NOTHING anyone could do about
it, but in the years after the war there were bomb
sites all over London that were places for boys to
play. I suppose, in theory, someone owned these houses.
Often there were fences put up round the houses, stout
fences, with padlocks at the gates and very clear warnings
as to how the buildings were unsafe and the authorities
took no responsibility for anyone breaking in. But the
truth is that some of these houses stayed like that for years.
No one could find their heirs, or those unlucky beneficiaries couldn't find the money for repairs. The government
had people to house and so it put up what we called "prefabs," which were long huts bolted together in sections,
and some of them erected in places where there had been
ruined houses. There were prefabs in our area that lasted
until the 1970s. Families put there in 1945 must have died
there and left the emergency boxes to their children. There
was a joke about how the government was sticking with

the prefabs because if there was another war they'd have saved money! We did mock our government, even though I realize now that the Attlee Labour government that came in in 1945 was probably the most important Britain has ever had.

But something was up. It was all very well, me being pushed forward in the crowds so that Mr. Churchill could smile at me, but at the end of that summer there was a general election and Labour beat the Tories up and down. It was a landslide. Grannie told me this was the treacherous ingratitude of the British public, and a shocking thing. Yet it had to come from the dreadful job Tory-type officers had done in the war, and before that, through the thirties, the impact of the Depression, which had hit the lower classes hardest of all. The soldiers coming back from the war had had enough of the old ways, even if Winnie had been a champion. Shyly, timidly, a lot of English people longed for something new. Two extraordinary wars had been fought in thirty years, and in a way one generation carried them both. The damage was everywhere to be seen, and somehow the patient herd of Britons waited to discover their reward or recompense. I suppose when it came it was to make Britain a modern country—tough, cynical, greedy, a version of wartime's black-market attitude—and it was the last thing many Britons wanted.

In summer, of course, we played on the streets. There was very little traffic. Kids roamed around the neighborhood without much fear, except for those bombed houses, where, sooner or later, the fence developed a hole and the word went around that we could get in. Our parents said we weren't to do it, and, naturally, we told them we wouldn't. And it was scary. But at one house I knew it was like this. You could get through the fence, and then there was a basement window that was out. With that, you were in the building, and you could study the hole that was in the middle of it and went three storeys high. A bomb had come in through the roof and blown out several floors. You could see the night sky, and we got ourselves torches so that we could find things like this: there was a desk in a corner in one room and there was a letter that had been in the process of being written and stopped in the middle. And in the time since no one had thought to take it away or post it or burn it. I heard stories about meals still on the table, but I never saw that, and I can't believe the rats would have allowed it. For Samuel Whiskers was there before us boys, and sometimes there were older kids who even reckoned to have lived in the house for a while. You climbed stairs at your peril. There were staircases that swayed like broken bridges and stopped in midair—like the staircase in *Kidnapped*! The living rooms were exposed to the night air, but sometimes suggested that the residents had just left for a moment, like stage sets waiting for the next act. But a stage where the curtain comes up, and the lights shine, but no one exits or enters. Imagine how closely you begin to look at that stage.

We boys passed on stories that people were killed in these bombed houses. After all, there might be unexploded bombs in the debris, shells buried but waiting. All over Britain there were mines and bombs like that, just waiting to be touched, to say nothing of the floor, which might creak and then fall through. There was one film, *The Yellow Balloon*, where a boy thinks he's caused the death of another kid on a bomb site, and another, *Hunted*, where Jon Whiteley is a boy who meets a man (Dirk Bogarde) hiding in a bombed house on the run.

You must not think that after a great war, life and the forms filled out for it all—the paperwork—slip back into place. After the war there were deserters and people who had gone into hiding for one reason or another. Or there would be just one person left from a family trying to find purpose again. From 1940 to 1945, the number of illegitimate births in Britain nearly trebled. People were slipping away. Bomb sites were places for them to hide and wait. And so they may have come into competition for the brief security. There was, as never before, a black market (which you didn't have to regard as crime, even if frightening people ran it), for the sale of nylons, a bottle of whiskey, or a bit more meat than the ration book allowed. Or fresh papers—there were people who had gone off the record-keeping system. I know a man who in 1945 or thereabouts started to live with another woman and got the papers for it—it was my dad. Do you think Harry Lime only lived in Vienna, or was less dangerous at home? I read recently that in Germany in the years after the war there were two million violent deaths. In arguments for a meal or a place to be. In the settling of scores, like wives killing husbands. These things happened, and the chaotic Germany gave a pass on them. The paperwork never caught up.

The number was nowhere near as large in Britain, because we had won, poor suckers, and because, after all, we were British, thank you very much, and we don't do that sort of thing, do we? But lives went away. My dad came back every Friday evening, but he might not have done. (His brother moved to Canada. His father died in his own bath.) And I wonder what my mum would have done, eventually. Would she have made a report and said she thought perhaps he lived near St. Albans? But there were double and triple lives then, the sport of war—or a liberty that war permitted—that was out of control.

Murders were talked about as if they were social events. I didn't know it then, but it was a great age of British writing—Graham Greene, Patrick Hamilton, Julian Maclaren-Ross—about brittle, broken people on the edges of society. And before that, the painter Walter Sickert had done extraordinary paintings of Camden murder mysteries: white bodies in rooms as dark as brown ale, in love or in the act of killing. They were the pictures that led to Bacon and Freud and Alfred Hitchcock, and they were a sure sign of the violence that wars had fostered in British people.

I was in a bombed house once in broad daylight, and it took me several minutes before I realized there was a man sitting hunched in an armchair. He didn't look at me, or move. He was totally indifferent to the fact that neither the house nor the chair was his. He didn't pounce on me. But a voice spoke.

"Whatyer, matey? Whatyer got?"

"Nothing," I said. (Don't talk to strangers, they said, but sometimes strangers were so ready to be friendly.)

"No good to me," he said. "You got a cup o' tea?"

"No," I said.

"A dripping sandwich?"

"No," I said.

He sighed, and made one last try. "A good cigar?"

Is it Pip and Magwitch? If I had had a Mars bar as a piece of cold pie for him, could I have inherited one day? I moved on, disappointed with myself. But the strange thing was how this man and I didn't have to fight for the room he was sitting in. We didn't have to go as far as murder.

"Where've you been, then?" It was Sally, studying me.

"I was at the chip shop," I said.

"You were not," she said. "Look at you—dust on your sleeve, in your hair. You were in the houses, weren't you?"

"Don't tell Mum," I said.

"Don't you worry about Mum yet," she said. "You worry about me."

"Whatyer going to do?"

"Smack your face, smarty-pants, that's what I'll do. Have you been told about the houses?"

"Yes."

"What were you told? Were you told, nod your head and say, 'Yes, silly,' and then go exploring in them? Were you?"

"Yes, Sally."

"Silly sod!" she said bitterly. "You don't deserve the caring. And you know what?"

"What?"

"No one cares if I go in the houses. No one cares about me."

"Do you go in the houses?" I asked. I knew she was brave.

"Worse," she said.

"You shouldn't go," I said. "Really, you shouldn't."

"You going to stop me?"

"Yes," I said. "I will."

"My hero," she said, and I knew she was being sour, but she wanted it.

You see, it was crazy, and it was just Grannie saying that Hitler might have been on Tooting Bec Common, but it wasn't ridiculous. Once in a while, they found a body on the Common. It would usually be a woman, and I gathered that women worked the Common. There was danger all around, and sometimes the greatest danger was just understanding what the grown-ups were talking about. It was as if the whole country was going to need time to get over the war. Those prefabs lasted much longer than the bomb sites. And Britain was a dodgy place until the late 1950s. People used to make jokes, with the rationing and all the shortages. "Good job we only won the war!" they said. "If we'd been triumphant, we'd be in the gutter now." And a few years after the war you'd hear people reminisce about the Dunkirk spirit—how, after Dunkirk, everyone had rallied round, doing their best to get along with everyone else so they'd have some sticks to beat Jerry with! But that spirit was gone by 1945, and the bombed houses were the emblem of an official life that had started up, and Dad was close enough to it to leave me wondering whether it wasn't the officialdom he had left as much as Mum and me. You see, I don't know that he'd ever really worked it out. Long after I was gone and Mum was dead, he'd come back sometimes and sit in his chair like that man in the house who only wanted a cup of tea. And I don't know why he did that if he didn't nurse some part of him that regarded the place as "home."

It could be madness—I never ruled that out—but it could be that he had a theory about the way he had been driven out, and had been a wanderer ever afterwards. Now, you may say that that's pretty far-fetched and just an example of how desperate I was—am—to retain his love, to explain him. Fair point. But it's a sign too of how when someone does a mad thing they leave you trying to explain it.

I asked my mum once why there were bombed houses so long after the war, because I knew there was a housing shortage, too. Reg and Trill lived in a tiny caravan for a while at the bottom of someone's garden, just to have a place. And Mum said she didn't know. It was "all wrong," she said, except that the houses made people remember the war. And in Europe, she said—Britain wasn't quite Europe then—"There are refugees all over the place, people living in camps who've lost their countries. So many people were lost in the war."

I asked, "Killed?" and she said not just that, but people whose stories had stopped, who found that the whole dream had broken in pieces. Had she loved him, and wanted him to stay? Then imagine that he'd never really been resolved to go away. It's the only thing that fits with bloody coming back. So I'm dreaming?

12

"ALL ROADS LEAD TO the ground," said Dad. He would usually say that around lunch-time on a Saturday. He'd spend the late morning at the stamp shop adding a few delicacies from the Seychelles and Montenegro to his collection, and I would often be there with him turning the stamps into a geography lesson. "Montenegro, alas, is no longer with us, gone the way of Bosnia-Herzegovina."

Then as the morning ended, he'd announce the program for the afternoon. And if I was lucky, we were headed for the Bridge, where Chelsea played. We would take the 49 bus and hop off it as it came to the north end of the Battersea Bridge and turned right onto Cheyne Walk. Already, we were in a scurry of people walking the extra distance to Stamford Bridge. That's when he told me to be brisk because "All roads lead to the ground!" The river was gray. The mist was sepia. The air was scathing, and if you blew your nose there was grime in the phlegm. This was

London, the center of it all, the Smoke, and the Flower Show, but the air was worse than in Streatham, and there was a smell on the raw breeze like that of blood. The expectation of the English soccer ground is more pungent than anything I know.

We had played soccer in the kitchen, and in the road outside the house, with just a tennis ball. It was the game, and you could get a feel for nineteenth-century London in a football ground surrounded by cheap, terraced housing just thrust down in the dense city. Dad had told me of a great game at the Bridge—it must have been 1946—when the Dynamo Moscow team came to Britain to play a few exhibition matches. It was as a thank you for the wartime alliance, even if that was going south fast. And it had marked the return of big games.

Except that the afternoon of this game there was a fog, what we called a pea-souper. That was a generous description, since pea soup was very good stuff and had a real green color to it. The pea-soup fog was yellow and brown. I suppose it was the sulphur, but it might just as well have been the shit. It was vile, and it was killing some of us. In the house next door to ours there was a man who coughed his guts out for half an hour every morning of his life before he could do anything else. He died, of course, in his fifties, some kind of bronchitis.

The Dynamo game was a big event, and the people at the Bridge said, "We've got to play it." There was a sell-out crowd and a rare sense of post-war fraternity. But from the middle of the pitch you couldn't see the goals. Special occasion, they decided. And then they let more people in. No one has ever explained it, but Chelsea had a running track and a dog track round the pitch then, and they let people sit on the ground. Stamford Bridge was supposed to hold 65,000. But they reckoned that 80,000 were there, seeing the ghosts glide through the smog, but not seeing the whole thing. Dad had been there (he claimed), and he said it was tremendously exciting, with Tommy Lawton lifting the Chelsea side to a narrow victory. And there were pictures in the paper of all the players—very awkward—giving bunches of flowers to each other before the game. Well, I had no way of knowing why I could not have been there, and I knew that Tommy Lawton was a great player, the one Dad often imitated in our games. So at last I got taken to see Chelsea.

The crowds were like nothing I had seen before. And in the crush getting into the ground Dad had to protect me and hold on to me. It was all men, and all in dark formal clothing—there were so few leisure clothes in those days. And there was a deep, stewed smell in the crowd that I'm sure was unwashed clothes, never mind about the men, the fags, and the matches. It was only when public smoking stopped that you realized how many people had smelled like death for years. And the crowd surged and fluctuated and there were often cries of "Hold on!" and "Wotch it, mate!" though the language as I recall was absolutely clean—the one thing that got washed. Sometimes a boy felt himself lifted off his own feet in those crowds and carried in the surge of motion.

There was the open terrace on one side of the ground, but Dad had got us seats in the new North Stand at a corner of the ground. This was providential because it gave us a lovely, high-angle view of the part of the pitch where a right-winger took on the full-back. I think it was 1948, and it was Chelsea vs. Blackpool. I was about to see Stanley Matthews, who had just joined Blackpool from Stoke City. He was capped for England before the war and was famous as the greatest ball controller in the game—he could dribble the ball up to an opponent and go round him, with the ball, leaving the opponent flat on his back or cast adrift. He was hunched, rather frail-looking, and his hair was receding.

Matthews had a routine. The ball would be passed to him and he'd face the Chelsea full-back. He'd stop in his tracks. The whole game would pause for its great show. Then Matthews would jink and side-step and do his magic, and as a rule he got past. There was already talk that his style was all very well, but rather show-offy and not the most effective way to play team soccer—especially not if you marked Matthews with a man who cut off the ball before it ever reached him. The great dogmas of work rate and finding space were hardly current yet, so for a moment Matthews's virtuoso balance won gasps and those rhythmic roars of delight such as you hear at a bullfight. Some full-backs weren't having it. They fouled Stanley, they pounded him. The Chelsea back that day—I don't know his name—was a servant of beauty. He waited to be defeated over and over again by this pale figure in a tangerine shirt, and at the end of the game the fans gave him a nice ovation for being such a good sport and a clean lad.

We waited in the seats when the game was over to let the crowds clear. And I hated the exit. On a Saturday evening, after the soccer, there was always greyhound racing at Stamford Bridge, and it was during the match that the dogs were delivered to the kennels. Well, the dogs were excited and the noise of the crowd only made them worse. So as you went past the kennels you got not just their howling but the benefit of the great loads of shit they were shifting. Still, it was sensible to wait. The crowd was so big and the buses—extra buses for game day—were passing the stops without any room. We always took two or three times as long to get home as we had to get there. But a big soccer match at the Bridge was the class of the game. In those days you were seeing the best players, national heroes, doing it on slavery contracts for no more than £15 a week. The live crowds were as big as the game has ever had in Britain, and there was no TV, no Match of the Day, with some soccer players as pundits and comics on the box.

But the size of the crowds daunted me. In fact, years later the rules for watching soccer in Britain changed when there was a disaster at Hillsborough. It was another big game, and the crowd on the terrace was surging. That's when you could get lifted up and trampled. At Hillsborough that day a barrier broke and something like a hundred people were killed. That's when a new law was passed that everyone at a game had to have a seat. So soccer was reformed. It became an expensive entertainment for richer people. And in the end the violence went out of the game, but not without a struggle. By then soccer players were super-stars from all over the world. But as late as the early '60s, if you went to see Chelsea you were watching South London kids who had been apprenticed to the club and who might play an entire career there. The loyalty and the identification were like gang warfare, though at that point no hint of violence had appeared in the crowds.

But in my first days, just after the war, you could believe that England was the stronghold of world soccer. In 1947, as another gesture to the end of the war, there was a game at Hampden Park (in Scotland, the biggest stadium in the country) where Great Britain beat the Rest of Europe 6–1. In 1948, in Turin, England beat Italy 4–0. In Lisbon they beat Portugal 10–0. And then in 1950, the World Cup resumed and it was confidently predicted—by Dad and other dads—that England were favorites. That Cup was played in Brazil, and everyone in England thought that it was a peculiar place to play a World Cup.

Never mind, we had a cracking team: it included Bert Williams as goalkeeper; Alf Ramsey at full-back; Billy Wright and Jimmy Dickinson in the half-back line; and a forward line that could choose from Stanley Matthews and Tom Finney (the best wingers in the world), Jack Milburn of Newcastle, Wilf Mannion, Roy Bentley of Chelsea, and Stan Mortensen of Blackpool.

That side was beaten at a jungle clearing called Belo Horizonte in front of ten thousand people, 1–0, by the United States.

It was regarded as a fluke and a freak—though it was like losing to American boxers. It was hardly believed.

In the next few years, the truth about soccer dawned. In 1954, Hungary came to Wembley, England's ground. Since that stadium opened in 1923, only Eire, the Republic of Ireland, had ever beaten England, and as in so many other respects the Republic of Ireland was supposed not to count.

The golden year was 1953—or so we were told. The very young Queen Elizabeth was crowned. Edmund Hillary (with Sherpa Tenzing) climbed Mount Everest. Stanley Matthews got a medal as Blackpool at last won the FA Cup. And England took the Ashes from Australia at the Oval, not held for twenty years. It was as if Buckingham Palace people had arranged the calendar. But the following year the "Mighty Magyars" thrashed England 6–3. Theirs was a team that included Puskás, Kocsis, Hidegkuti, Czibor, Bozsik—great players, in a military attacking system. Players changed positions, and so evaded their set defenders. It was the turning point at which England had to see that soccer was not just strength, courage, or Englishness. It was a brain game in which there might be a system as well as bravery, perseverance, luck, and magic. In a return match, in Budapest, the Hungarians won 7–1.

Soccer might be art.

"Hey, Mum, that's not fair!"

13

IF GOD CALLED IT "sport" we gave it a try. We went to Gaelic football and speedway. I saw Reg Harris cycling at Herne Hill and I loved the way the cyclists climbed into the camber of the track in their effort to stay motionless before surrendering to a savage sprint attack. We went into some churchy parlor where a green table was stretched out in the light. A natty little man in a bow tie and a black waistcoat strolled around the table and the reds and the colors made dainty journeys to the corners. "Joe Davis," whispered Dad. A master and a god—and why not imagine God in his six-day work doing it at a table with a cue stick? We even saw a game of baseball, played by American military teams, and decided it was a dud. Lucky for the Americans they had never had to face the real sports of England.

But it was not just the watching. Long before I was able to perform, Dad had me out on the Common with a ball, a bat, and rackets. We used to get equipped for half a dozen sports. And on Tooting Bec Common in those days—provided and maintained by the LCC—there were grass tennis courts where I played. Dad was a very good tennis player. He found a light racket—wooden, of course—for me. He shortened my grip and taught me how to move to the ball. I couldn't serve, and I tried to run round my backhand, but we rallied, and I noticed the extra speed of the ball on grass.

This real play was added to by our regular trip to Wimbledon on the first Saturday of the fortnight. We went early, with a picnic, queued and always got good seats on court number 2. These were the days of great Australian players—Bromwich, Sedgeman, and McGregor—and we went for several years. Our last year was the first visit by a new generation of Aussies, Lew Hoad and Ken Rosewall, teenagers who seemed superior to their parents.

My favorites, though, were Jaroslav Drobny, who went from being Czech to Egyptian in one year—such were the vagaries of nationality—and a very elegant American, Budge Patty. (I'm sure it was the name that first drew me to him—he lived in Paris and seemed like a character out of *Tender Is the Night*.) One year, late in the afternoon, we left court 2 and took the chance of picking up spare seats on the Centre Court. After five p.m. anyone could fill them. We were there in the hallowed place watching two Americans, Shirley Fry and Louise Brough, and realized that the Centre Court was really different. The overhang roof that gave way to openness changed the light and the sound so that it felt indoors with just an extra soft light falling on the court. Whether a tennis court or a small stadium, the atmosphere was special. Years later, in September 1975, I walked into Fenway Park in Boston for the first time one night and had the same confusion about whether it was indoors or outdoors.

There was another thing about tennis. It was the space allowed to women. I think the first time I noticed anything that might be called sex was at Wimbledon watching a player called Kay Stammers. She was lean and dark and I thought she looked like my mother. She was also very tan and I noticed that when she stretched for a shot and her skirt swirled the tan went all the way up her legs to the white underpants. As if a bell had sounded, signaling my interest, tennis itself changed. An American player hit town, Gorgeous Gussie Moran, and she had the idea that if your underpants were going to show—and they were— well, give the public a thrill. She wore show pants, frilled pants, pink bow panties, knickerbocker glory panties— what you might even begin to think of as lingerie. I was moved, and I began to collect pictures of the players that you could purchase at Wimbledon: Pauline Betz, Doris Hart, Pat Todd, Nancy Chaffee. I bought pictures of the guys, too, with my pocket money, but it was the girls I was collecting, and so I learned to be nonchalant and resigned when court 2 followed a dramatic men's singles with a ladies doubles match.

Decades later there was a film I loved—Godard's *Pierrot le Fou*—in which the narrator's voice said something about how as Velázquez grew older he painted nothing but the spaces between things (the nervous system of movies). And the image cut to a girl playing tennis running in a set court, this way and that, reaching, stretching, keeping the ball in play. And somehow being as lovely as she can manage. Rallying. And my mind went back to those first intimations of sexuality and the feeling for an athlete at their best.

In those days, the next best thing to watching tennis was going to athletics. Dad would take me to the big events at the White City: Oxford vs. Cambridge; the Inter-Counties Championships; the AAA; and then the international matches. I loved to run, and was fast as a boy, so this was a great source of pleasure. It was there that we first saw Roger Bannister run, as well as McDonald Bailey and Arthur Wint, black men living in London, it was explained. Bailey was an explosive sprinter who had qualified to run for Britain in the 1948 Olympic Games, while Wint was a Jamaican, so tall he had an eight-foot stride that carried him in apparent slow motion.

In those days, the chief target in track athletics was for someone to run the mile in under four minutes. I remember seing Bill Nankeville win the Inter-Counties mile in 4 minutes, 8.8 seconds. That was getting close to the world-record times run by two Swedes, Gunder Hagg and Arne Andersson. There was also the English runner Sydney Wooderson, who looked like a railway booking clerk. My father raised the possibility that "young Bannister" might do it one day. He won the mile every year for Oxford and one year, lo and behold, after his race Bannister came into the stands with his parents, close to where we were sitting. I got a piece of paper and asked for his autograph. He laughed out loud at my request—perhaps it was the first time he had been asked—and signed for me.

We went to Wembley for one day of the 1948 Olympics. It was very warm and the crowd was huge. I wanted McDonald Bailey in the 100 meters and we were there the day of that final. They were off and everyone stood up. I was too small to see anything. But I heard the feet on the cinders go past and Dad had to tell me that "Mac" was last. I know the finishing order still: Harrison Dillard; Barney Ewell; Lloyd La Beach of Panama; McCorquodale of Britain; Mel Patton; and Bailey.

The same day, in the heats of the 5000 meters we saw Emil Zátopek, the most extraordinary runner of the time, and Fanny Blankers-Koen, the Dutch woman who won every event she competed in.

Bannister was aimed at the 1952 Olympic Games in Helsinki. He was a favorite to win the 1500 meters but came in fourth. Dad said he had been out-thought in the race and hadn't used his ability to the best. I stayed following athletics in a time when I was running myself, and doing well enough. I used to train and run on the Common every evening. I even read articles about "interval training" and tried to copy it myself.

Then one morning in May 1954 I opened the paper and Bannister had done it: 3 minutes, 59.4 seconds, on a rainy evening at Iffley Road, Oxford. It was a minor track meeting, but Bannister had had his friends Chris Brasher and Chris Chataway with him as pacemakers. This was dubious, legally—was it a proper race with everyone running to win? Not really. Still, there had been enough timekeepers there and the record would stand.

Of course, I hadn't seen it—there was no way of seeing it unless you had been at Oxford that night. Then one day not long afterwards my mother and I were in Pratt's, the big store in Streatham, in the furniture department.

"Want to see something?" one of the clerks asked me.

"All right," I said.

The store had a new line of goods that was being sold in the furniture department: television sets. I had seen one the previous year when Grandma got a set—brand-new and very temperamental—for the coronation of the Queen. And I had cycled over in pouring rain to watch that. It seemed to go on all day, and fifty-three years later it is still the last coronation.

But the television at Pratt's went for just 3 minutes, 59.4 seconds, and then some extra as Bannister collapsed. It was the film of the race. It was painfully simple. The men just ran round the track. By the third lap it was clear that Chataway was nearly dying to keep up the pace and then on the last lap Bannister went free and ran into his own wall of pain and disbelief. And history.

I knew already that great achievement at sports was fueled not just by talent, but by need. Dad had a view of boxing, that it was for the underprivileged people in the world—above all, in his time, the blacks. People hurt in such drastic ways in life were hardened against damage in the ring. You had to be hungry, rough, coarse, uneducated. It is a good theory. But Roger Bannister was a boy like me: middle-class, nicely brought up, sent to a good school, and so on. His parents had been in the stands just a few rows away, eating hard-boiled eggs like us, with little squibs of foil paper filled with salt. Bannister was bright, well-spoken, polite. There was no killer instinct. He wrote about running very well later—in the spirit of a young doctor and a polar explorer—and it was clear that the four-minute mark was a barrier in his mind. And a challenge he took personally. In the last hundred yards it looked as if he was going to collapse and he talked about being in some other zone, deprived of oxygen, ecstatic yet desperate. Was that what glory was? And was it accessible for some nicely brought-up boy? Such questions preoccupied me. But the drama and the headlong imagery of his run were amazing. Was he escaping, or running toward something? For that last two hundred yards he had been so alone. And I felt lucky that someone had thought to film it. Though the film had made decisions: it was a documentary record, shot from a car circling the running track. For the most part it was a single shot. And the refusal, or the inability, to cut was vital to Bannister's passion. I was crying, for Bannister, for running (which I loved for its own sake), and for man getting closer to . . . to what? To zero? But I think I saw even then that you could make kids cry just by running, or by deciding where to put the camera.

"There you are," said the man in the store. "Buy a television set and you can watch that sort of thing all the time."

I nodded grimly and said, "It's not a very good picture, though."

"What do you mean?" he said, aghast.

"You can see the lines," I said. "It's not like cinema, is it?"

"This will make mincemeat of cinema," said the man in an aggrieved way.

14

"HE LIKES IT," said my mum. "He likes it very much, but it upsets him." And so it does, still. What else do you expect out of life? But what part of life was she talking about?

I loved sports and still do, and there was a brief period in my life when I kidded myself that I might be good enough. The thought was nonsense. I was a middling all-round talent. I had an eye for a ball. I was fast. There are millions like that, and if we're lucky we go on dreaming till we drop, and we're shy if we ever meet the real thing. Going to the Bridge once, Dad and I found ourselves walking beside one of the players. Never mind who it was. And Dad tried talking to him—for my sake, I'm sure. But the bloke hadn't got two words. No small talk, let alone stories of the big game. To this day I know few things more crushing than having to listen to geniuses (with their feet) trying to say what it felt like. Don't worry, I'll tell them what it felt like, because I was imagining it all.

. . .

BUT THERE WAS ANOTHER PLACE, and there I had a chance.

For years, I knew the residential roads, the Common and the High Road in Streatham and not much else. And there was a shop for everything on the High Road, a hundred small establishments with a fixed staff selling everything from bread and pastries to books, fruit and vegetables, records, cosmetics, lipstick, sheet music, coffee, and toys. There was nothing yet in the late '40s of the supermarket or one-stop shopping. Streatham in its time would be nearly ruined by the absence of parking on the High Road. By the late '50s as people got cars they went to the new markets, where you could park. These were built on the edges of towns. The specialty shops of Streatham—to which everyone walked—were killed by the changing trade.

There were only a very few large buildings on the High Road: the railway stations, Streatham and Streatham Hill; the bus depot at Telford Avenue; the several churches in a kind of throttled Gothic; the library; and the cinemas. When my mother took me shopping in the mornings, those cinemas were the special, alluring places because they were not open yet. Their heavy glass doors turned at midday, but at nine or ten the places that did nocturnal trade were "resting," sleeping in late, while servants cleared away the night's garbage and freshened the air with scented sprays. The cinemas smelled pretty, like women, and despite the scale of their buildings there was no question about their gender.

Another point struck me. Go to a regular store and you had something solid—a pound of sugar, a yard and a half of fabric, a hammer—wrapped up in paper. But if you went to the cinemas, you came away with nothing solid or wrapped. It was just that your head was blown up like a balloon.

Moreover, the cinemas were immensely decorated, utterly beyond the limits of realism or the lifelike. I had been inside English churches and I abided by their rather harsh self-illustration; if that was the story they wanted to tell, so be it. Church paintings and stained glass aspired to one gloomy message. But the decor in cinemas was crazed and extravagant, and perfect preparation for the films or the pictures. I never thought at the time that the messages of church and cinema were in competition. What chance did the churches have? But I see now how they employed the same way of referring to "another place" or a "once upon a time" so much more vivid than life. I gathered that if you accepted God you were safe for the future, whatever safe was. But it was no contest for me. The cinema had girls and action and music I loved. Everyone involved with the churches of the world had good reason to be alarmed when the movies came in. Whatever his virtues or game plan, God made a big mistake when he first messed with temptation. He should have made us differently or learned to get on with human nature.

I asked what happened inside these cinemas and Mum said, well, it was a bit like theater. That was a reasonable answer, of course, and not simply wrong. But I felt an early distinction. In the theater, the pigeons were real; they left droppings where they had been. And the people were solid and ready to ask you what you thought. They were as intimidating as the Grand Vizier.

The people in pictures did not know I was there. I worked this out gradually, and I came to see it as their great kindness. They could be seen in the distance first where they were active and heroic, but then, as if by magic, they came right up to the screen, so you could see their faces, and they were lovely, all of them, not just the women. Even the men had a shining look that made me want to be them or be with them. Their features were attractive and the faces vivid. They were to be seen. And often they were very good or very bad so you knew what to think of them.

"Where are they?" I asked, looking around the large premises. These suburban theaters were big. They had an upstairs and a downstairs and they must have held at least fifteen hundred people. Morever, in those days they were always packed.

"They're not here," I was told. Indeed, ever after, as if to make that plain lie acceptable—because they *were* here and they were mine and they waited to let me look at them—I was told they were "in America." As a child, I confused the two terms—"in the movies" and "in America." And it is only with time that I have come to see how important and creative that confusion is. Of course, what the confusion has done to that unlucky breed of ghost, Americans, is another matter, and I doubt I will live long enough to work it out.

"Well, if they're not here," I argued, "what is happening?"

It's a tough question and one that the people who run the churches have just as much trouble answering as parents with a child on their lap in a cinema. Dad said that the whole thing was on film and there was a man upstairs who turned a handle and the story unfolded. He pointed up to a small bright square window in the back of the cinema, and I perceived that a flood of light or a beam from that window reached to the screen. In those days that beam of light was thick with writhing smoke since everyone at the movies smoked. Projection. The image. The tiny rectangle of celluloid—these were not explained. And so a miracle was occurring and really it was every bit as potent—in which these men, their horses, their range, their America, were up on a screen far larger than life. I knew of only two experiences that were really like what happened in the cinema—not theater, not being read to, but radio and dreaming. The latter was the most suggestive because while the dream might be very exciting, or frightening, I was there at its lip without being noticed. I was infinite and the light was my fantasy. Put it like that, I suppose, and the whole thing should have been stopped in 1905.

Like everyone else, you might well ask me, "Well, what film did you see first?" I don't exactly know. I was more aware of the process at first than the particular titles or series. But a very early picture was Laurence Olivier's *Henry V*, which opened in Britain in 1945. I do recall seeing that and being told by Dad that it was one more thing that stood for "our" victory in the war. The film was a great occasion, and in seeing it I was doing my duty. Do I hear or imagine parental amens about the experiment, or how is the boy expected to understand Shakespeare? I think there was a dispute and I believe my dad talked me through the film as best he could. Still, I know I was bewildered by the gift of tennis balls for people going to war.

What I recall is the face of Olivier just as he goes onstage as the King. If you remember, the movie begins at the old Globe Theater with an audience and players both about to do *Henry V*. Somehow I got that. But after that I was at a loss until the battle and the sound of English arrows in what was actually an Irish sky. And then it happened. I saw the faces of boys burning in the screen.

This is not in the film. Of course, it could be now. The idea that we might have to see live flesh burning is no longer monstrous. In 1945 no one would have allowed it. Still, there is a moment when the French raid the English camp, when a group of page boys are described as having been killed. Burned alive. I saw it, and in 1945 in a packed theater I started crying violently and my dad had to carry me out of the theater, no doubt to the scathing comments that it was ridiculous to take a four-year-old boy to see a film like this.

My parents reassured me that I could not have seen what I described. The futility of that argument! We see what we see. Seven or eight years later I was in a class called upon to see the film of *Henry V* as a help in Shakespeare studies. I was afraid but curious. So I watched carefully and found that I had been told the truth. One did not see burning faces.

About forty years later I was living in San Francisco with a young son, Nicholas. He was an enthusiast of films on tape. We had a library of them. His mother and I had chosen a range of films that might be suitable for him. I was in the next room as he watched *Henry V*. And he came into my office in quiet tears. He had seen something "horrible." Faces burning. It seemed like a ghost story. But later

I looked at the film very carefully. It was the same work from 1945. But here was the thing Olivier had done, and I do not blame him. He had a shot of page boys asleep. Their faces. A tent. And a little later the tent on fire. If the images don't melt, or dissolve, the montage does. Don't tell children they have not seen something in a medium as wild and poetic as the movies. Do not tell them that they have got it wrong in reading the meanings in life. They have only their eyes and feelings to go on. And there were men on the street, their faces like Asian masks, the skin stretched, the eyes at odd angles. These were plastic-surgery faces after a cockpit of fire or a tank hit by an artillery shell.

15

"ONE THING ABOUT THAT LAD," said Grandma, "you can always take him to see a picture. Then he's happy for a couple of hours."

Did that mean that otherwise I was unhappy or difficult? It didn't seem that way to me. Though I had got into the habit of screaming the house down and saying no, I wouldn't go to school, to such an extent that it no longer looked like a passing phase. I was against school. But the family rallied round my mother, I think. There was distress that Dad had left her, bewilderment that he hadn't quite completed the shift, and every urge to make things easier for "Non." In time she got a part-time secretarial job in London on Oxford Street, and I became a latchkey kid. With this extra. That I took the bus to school, got off, took another bus, and came back home. Grannie was there, of course, though her health was slipping fast.

"Aren't you well?" she'd ask as I came in at the front door.

"Not really," I'd say, and I would go up to our flat and listen to the radio. Sometimes after lunch she'd take me off to a film. And when Mum got back from work, her face would sink and that worried look would come over her. "You have to go to school," she'd say. "And I have to go to work. So you've got to get on with it."

But in half an hour she'd have forgiven me and would be cooking dinner. That evening she'd write the note to the school saying I had been sick. But then sometimes I didn't go the next day either.

"What did you see at the pictures?" she asked.

"I don't know what it was called," I said.

"What was it about?"

"I don't quite know."

Grannie liked grown-up films with unkind ladies— Bette Davis, Joan Crawford. I could never quite work out their problems.

"Was it suitable?" asked Mum.

"Oh yes," I said, never knowing what she meant.

So I went all the time. I liked Westerns and adventure films, but I would take anything. It was the being there that I liked. In the same period of time I saw two pictures that referred to St. Louis. There was a Western, *South of St. Louis*, with Joel McCrea and Zachary Scott, and then there was *Meet Me in St. Louis*. My mum took me to that one on her own, as if it were for us. And I loved the idea of the big family of three generations living in one house, bright in the summer sun.

"Where is St. Louis?" I asked, and I noticed that its name shifted from Lewis to Louis.

"In America," said Mum. "In the middle."

Don't tell me you can't learn from a film (and people did try to tell me that). In *Meet Me in St. Louis*, I understood the family tension that the dad works in a bank and the bank wants him to go to New York. The family of the girls—it was a girl film—pretend to be very happy about this, but really they want to stay in St. Louis. Because it's home and where their friends are. Then at the Christmas just before they are to leave it all comes out. Esther sings "Have Yourself a Merry Little Christmas" to Tootie, but the younger girl is so unhappy she smashes the snowmen in the garden. The dad hears this and realizes he can't go to New York. He can't leave.

Years later, I marvel at this un-American attitude, the not going to New York, not taking a chance, and the adventure. But I realize that the movie was made in 1944, so it was saying to people away from home, Don't worry. Home will be as you left it. We are all coming home. (Unless there's a hole in the ground where home was.)

"My dad goes away," I said to my mum. I suppose I had noticed.

"That's right," said Mum. "But we're still here." Yes, that was true, and I felt safe, I suppose, though I was afraid that someone who we needed with us went away every Monday morning. Yes, he came back with terrific jokes that seemed to last all weekend. But I had noticed, and I couldn't guess why no one else in the family had.

Best of all in the film was Esther, a version of my Sally, the older sister who would take care of you, with eyes that ached to be loved as much as Judy Garland's trembly voice begged for it. I liked the way that women sang from a very early age, and I was torn between the purity of Doris Day and the yearning in Judy Garland. Between "Over the Rainbow" and "The Man That Got Away" lay my childhood and Judy's life. I still have a dream in which I am a songwriter and I walk into some scruffy dive one night and there in front of hardly a soul is this lost girl singing one of my songs. So I take her in hand and offer a little advice on phrasing, and soon we are acting out the song.

For those few years after the war, I became if not Oliver Twist at the pictures then the Artful Dodger. When I skipped school, I would walk around, exploring, waiting for the cinemas to open. After that, I depended on the certificate of the film. If it was a U I could go in on my own, using my school dinner money. But if the film was an A— and I was beginning to discover that most interesting films were As—then I needed an adult to accompany me. So I asked strangers, accosted on the steps to the box office, whether they would take me in with them.

Yes, my mum learned that I was doing this. I daresay parents could be reported to the Social Services for such neglect or risk taking. But strangers let me ride along with them, and nothing ever happened beyond my going out with a group of old ladies afterwards. We went to the restaurant in Pratt's. They had tea and cakes and I had an ice cream. They asked me what I had thought of the picture and I tried to give an account—it was the beginnings of criticism. Of course, I was upset and afraid quite often, and I think it is necessary for us to remember that, even surrounded by the branches of his family, a child is alone in the dark confronted by the great wonder of a screen many times his own size.

I saw *Scott of the Antarctic*. I was eager to see it because

I knew the story already. And there came a scene where the men were in their tent eating their grim meal and one of them threw up—it was enough, I was in tears, ready to be extensively sick myself, and hustled out of the theater by whichever relative had taken me. Somehow I saw *The Red House*, in which the house itself was mysterious and filled with demons and surprises. It was Edward G. Robinson, and I had nightmares of his strange swollen face twisted in fear or malice. Who could be sure which it was? Of course, I should not have been there. I should have been at school. But today I could go into raptures about the strange screen persona Robinson had. He was nasty and frightening sometimes, but he was also a very ordinary little man. I saw *The Flame and the Arrow* and *Captain Horatio Hornblower*, two robust adventures wherein I placed myself in dreams and daydreams that can extend the films' stories. Inevitably, in that predicament, I fell violently in love with Virginia Mayo, who happened to be the female lead in both films.

Grannie took me to see *The Third Man*. I didn't understand it, but I was in constant fear from its sinister Viennese atmosphere. And then, very late in the film, Harry Lime, or Mr. Orson Welles, appeared. Grannie reached out her cold three-fingered hand and held my wrist and announced, "Here comes a very bad man."

It was a valiant try on her part, and well meant. But as the cat curled on Lime's feet in the doorway, I was with the cat. And when the light from a room upstairs fell on Welles's face and he grinned at us all, I was sure he had seen me—just like Winnie in the street. I believed then, and I have only enriched the point of view after a book on Welles and seminars on him, that this immense talent and personality began with the idea of a boy dressing up to look like a grown man. Lime was by all agreement a wicked man, but Orson's smile was so appealing. I was not in the least surprised when, within a year or two, Orson as Harry Lime was back in a radio series and Lime was a Robin Hood character, or worthy company for Dick Barton, Special Agent.

I laughed myself helpless at Bob Hope. I was ready to catch Burt Lancaster on the trapeze of adventure. My mother and I used to go to Anna Neagle pictures, content with their loveliness and their blithe references to Park Lane and Mayfair (the purple properties in Monopoly). In these films Ms. Neagle found lovely clothes and happiness— often with Michael Wilding, the tuberose among actors— in a world of luxury apartments and ravishing ease. My mum was quite candid about wanting to live in that "pretty" world. She carried no hint of class grievance. A year or two later, the semiconscious raptures of close-ups in *A Place in the Sun* drove me to try reading Theodore Dreiser and there I began to feel the throb of envy or resentment. But was it unfair that only some were rich and pretty? Or was it just hard luck? It was a few more years still before I read my first Hemingway, *The Sun Also Rises,* and I caught the whip of irony in "Wouldn't it be pretty to think so?" I still use that phrase.

I remember all these pictures, and many others, but nothing was like the experience of seeing *Red River.* Long before it opened, I was ready to see it. There must have been ads or previews in *Film Fun,* and I had adopted a policy with advertising of complete obedience. It was a Western—the biggest of them all, it was said.

Well, as it happened, my aunt Trill was the one who had the good luck, or whatever it was, to take me to *Red River*.

"Oh, it's black-and-white," she said, as it came on. She sounded disappointed.

"They only did black-and-white in those days," I said with a mixture of nonsense and authority that the critic should master early. And then we hushed as the film began.

It is the story of a man, Tom Dunson, part of a wagon train going west. There are Indians about, but Dunson and his friend, Groot, leave the wagons and follow Dunson's instinct to go south into Texas. Indians attack the wagon train, and Dunson soon finds a girl's bracelet on an Indian he kills. Dunson and Groot find a boy—Matthew Garth—wandering in the wilderness, the only survivor from the wagon train. They come to the Rio Grande and stop there, but only after Dunson has won the land from two Mexicans. A great ranch is built.

The film sighs, and fifteen years pass. The Civil War has been fought. Dunson has a great herd of cattle but nothing to do with it. He has heard there is a rail line in Kansas or Missouri, if they could drive the cattle that far. But Dunson is older, more severe, gray haired, meaner. He is John Wayne as no one had ever seen him before. And Matthew Garth is no longer a boy—he is Montgomery Clift. They will lead the cattle drive north.

It is a hard journey on which Dunson grows harder. In the end, Matthew leads the mutiny against him. He takes over the herd and leaves a wounded Dunson to follow as he wishes. Soon the journey is a pursuit, and Tess Millay appears, a girl encountered on another wagon train. She loves Matthew, but she's ready to give herself to Dunson to save the boy.

They reach Abilene, with its railroad. The cattle will be sold in a great deal. Everybody is happy, but everyone knows Dunson is coming beneath a vengeful cloud. The story ends on the streets of Abilene, and I won't tell you how. Anyone who gives a story away is unfit to handle story.

Now, I am not the only one here who may tell you that *Red River* is one of the classic movies. Still, I am the only one who can have a chance of conveying what it meant to me. I did not want the limited conclusion (grand as it is); I wanted the cattle drive to last in time. I loved the story and I can see no alternative to the way I "identified" with a struggle between a father and a son. Dunson and Garth were not blood related, and their toughness and resolve kept them apart, but they saw themselves as linked. The grown man needed a rebel son. The son needed a teacher. And it was obvious they were going to clash and think about killing each other. This was the first story I had encountered that I knew was meant for me. So I could not give it up.

"I want to see it again," I told my aunt Trill.

"You've just seen it," she said. "You know what happens. It won't be any different next time."

"I just want to stay there," I said.

"There?"

I nodded at the screen, but I meant the valley where they rode and the community of the men. It was a place I longed to be, in the picture, a part of it.

She told me I could come again, with Mum or Dad, but

I would not budge. At last, she agreed. She had shopping to do. I could see the film again and she would be back in time so that as the film ended I was to be in the lobby waiting for her. She stood and left me there.

Films then were in "continuous performance." People were leaving and arriving and the girl with the tray of ice cream and drinks was standing in her spotlight. Then I felt another light brush across my face. It was an usherette's torch. It was Sally!

"Where've you been?" I called out.

"I got a job," she said—the woman of the world. "So, you like this one?"

"Oh, yes," I said. "I'm seeing it again!"

"Know how many times I've seen it?" she asked. "Thirty-one. No, I tell a lie, it's thirty-two."

I was amazed.

"Why do you like it, then?" she asked.

"Matthew," I said, like a team supporter.

"But don't you like Dunson, too?"

"Well," I said.

"Come on," said Sally, "they're alike."

"Not really."

"They're so alike it hurts them to look at each other," she said. "Anyway, you all right here, on your own?"

"Yes," I said.

"OK, sprout. If you need me, you just whistle. You know how to whistle?"

16

WHAT DID SALLY MEAN about Dunson and Garth being hardly able to look at each other? I saw the film, and I had found the Red River on maps, so I had an inkling of "where" it happened. I had a favorite book, a history of the Wild West, in which a strange ghost boy took a couple of living boys on a tour of great moments in Western history. I imagined myself as part of the trail crew in that dawn before Dunson set off, with Wayne riding down from the ranch house in the early light and saying, "Take 'em to Missouri, Matt." I said, "Take 'em to Missouri, Matt," over and over again, and I suppose I was working on an American accent.

At Rosemead, there was an elocution class so that we might all lose that lazy South London accent (the way I talked in the streets and in the bombed houses) that sounds like a whine and drops its g's. So I had thought about voice and speaking "properly." It was the first suggestion I ever had that you could alter your own voice. "Take 'em to

Missouri, Matt," as if Missouri were right around the corner and not a thousand miles away. There was the soft
stress on the name. People in films, I found, used names
more often than people in life, and in my England hardly a
real name was used. Everyone had diminutive nicknames,
knocking them down to size. "Take 'em to Missouri,
Matthew." You could go that way, by formal, or biblical,
names. And not using the name "Garth" confers responsibility—after all, Matthew will, literally, take the herd
away from Dunson. "Take 'em," as if it were going to be
no great problem, or nothing that men like these would
ever rate as a problem. "Take 'em," as in ride along with
them. Just show them the way.

And the peaceful, half-sleepy way in which Wayne
spoke. Wayne was an extraordinary actor, working at his
craft while the world had no inkling of its existence—
"Take 'em to Missouri, Matt," as if all the huge effort and
turmoil of the journey were like a dream, and just as
smooth. And as if Dunson were in no mood to wake the
cattle too soon—let the great rousing cries follow him.

I won't say the line again, but you may smile to learn
that I have a son called Mathew. Moreover, I have English
children and American children, and they both feel that I
speak with a peculiar accent. But I was raised in a generation of mid-Atlantic voices, from Cary Grant and Bob
Hope to Alistair Cooke, and already in the late '40s I had
found Cooke's exquisite *Letter from America* on BBC
radio, a steady report in which love or skepticism never got
quite the upper hand. (That show began in 1946, but it
only took on *Letter from America* as its title in 1950.)
What else does love need to be so loyal? How did Cooke

seem so gentle, so wise, and so wry unless it was because of his adopted regimen: England and America mixed and off-setting, like Scotch on the rocks? I had heard the poetic English voice—it was Olivier as Henry V, royal language—but I loved the easy conversational tone (the way Jimmy Stewart talked to Harvey, refusing to be astonished that a rabbit might be a good listener). I loved the declaratory English voice, but I loved even more the American surmise that is still working things out. To this day, the English self-confidence is repugnant to me, and it is shamed by the quiet American examination of doubt.

The first day I arrived in America (in 1973) there had been a flood in Maine, a summer flood. It was on the evening news and the Boston reporter, all quickfire and soft soap, had lined up an elderly Maine fellow to see if he had ever seen anything like this before. "Well, Mr. Parsons," he said. "I understand you've lived all your life in Maine." And the old-timer said, "Not yet."

In recent years a great deal of what I have done has been a matter of wondering whether I write English or American—or whether I need to be an actor to do either convincingly. And I still wonder whether "Not yet" was wicked old Herb Parsons putting his finger in Boston's eye, or a ninety-year-old too polite to say what a damn stupid question that was.

In British films, the people talked as if they wanted to cram every last word in even if it was a love story and they were Trevor Howard and Celia Johnson. There was an edge of desperation or hysteria in their Home Counties voices (as if passion might rip apart enunciation) and these lovers were recorded as if they were in wooden boxes. The sound in American films, the voice, was different. We could go into a chapter of technical stuff here, but in America they recorded talk as if it were discourse happening inside your own head—or between people in bed. People knew how to talk quietly, listening for the wind in the background or the sound of the cattle or the money grazing.

HIM: You really don't know who I am?

HER: You told me your name, Mr. Parsons. I'm awfully ignorant. I guess you caught on to that. You know, I bet I've heard your name a million times.

HIM: But you really like me, though, even though you don't know who I am?

HER: Oh, I surely do. You've been wonderful. Gee, without you, I don't know what I would have done. Here I was with a toothache, and I don't know many people.

HIM: I know too many people. I guess we're both lonely. You want to know what I was going to do tonight, before I ruined my best Sunday clothes?

HER: I bet they're not your best Sunday clothes. You've probably got a lot of clothes.

HIM: No, I was just joking. I was on my way to the Western Manhattan Warehouse, in search of my youth. You see, my mother died, a long time ago. Well, her things were put in storage out west. There wasn't any other place for them. I thought I'd send for them now. Tonight I was going to take a look at them. A sort of sentimental journey. I run a couple of newspapers. What do you do?

HER: Me?

HIM: Hmm. How old did you say you were?

HER: Oh, I didn't say.

HIM: I didn't think you did. If you had I wouldn't have asked you again, because I'd have remembered. How old?

HER: Twenty-two in August.

HIM: That's a ripe old age. What do you do?

HER: Oh, I work at Seligman's. I'm in charge of the sheet music.

HIM: That what you want to do?

HER: No, I wanted to be a singer, I guess. That is, I didn't. My mother did.

HIM: What happened to the singing?

HER: Well, Mother always thought—she always talked about grand opera for me. Imagine! Anyway, my voice isn't that kind. It's just as well, you know what mothers are like.

HIM: Yes.

"Take me out to the Western Manhattan Warehouse, Matt." It doesn't matter yet if you don't know where that dialogue is from—and I'll tell you later and tell you now that I made one change in the text to make a game out of it. But that's American talk, it's very natural seeming, yet it aspires to the whole picture and the entire inside deal in a lovely casual way that is free from underlining note. It's as if in a free country and a visual medium people were effortlessly revealing of themselves without being boastful or conscious of being in a story. It's movie talk, by which I mean that it has been recorded very "intimately," and in a mutual agreement by which each party consents to help open the other one up. When Elizabeth Taylor looks into the room where Montgomery Clift is alone shooting pool in *A Place in the Sun,* and she sees the tail end of his private trick shot, she says, "Wow!" and that's all it needs to put the oiled key in his shy lock. She might as well have put her hand in his pants, or his in hers.

This is not necessarily the way people talk in life. It's the kind of talk that befits a dream based on the hope for love. I always liked it in movies as much as the close-ups, the panoramas, and the music that ran from one to the other like a river, like Red River. It's a hint of what is to come— like the way I'm asking you to read—that I fell in love with intimate fluency just as I began to lose the hope of it.

17

THERE CAME A CHRISTMAS when my father asked me if I wanted to put on a show. I was about ten. What he was thinking of was that we'd present a play for the family get-together at Christmas, in the afternoon after the big Christmas meal. We'd learn lines and wear costumes and act it out. Of course, I agreed. It seemed like destiny. He suggested we do something from *Macbeth*. He read the opening of the play to me, the scene where Macbeth meets the three witches and they predict what will happen. I would be Macbeth, and he would be all the witches rolled into one. He did this for me. He thought of it. He worked it out. Do you see how much I loved him?

At the time, it was also justified as something to help my elocution class, and what it revealed was that I had early signs of a stammer. It was suggested that recitation would help. I hardly noticed the stammer yet, and only thought what tremendous fun to be Macbeth. Dad typed out the text we'd use and I think it was a skillful adaptation of Shakespeare. When we began to learn our lines, I found I could take them in very fast, even if some of the words had to be explained to me. We rehearsed at weekends, and Dad told me how to stand up straight and tall as Macbeth because he was a warrior, but how the man was afraid of the witches just because what they suggested was so close to his heart.

I don't think our "play" lasted more than ten minutes. I wore a tartan kilt, a white shirt, and a tam-o'-shanter, and I had a fire poker as my sword. Dad wore a filthy old shawl and generally overdid the disgustingness of the witches as best he could. He reveled in the ingredients that the witches used to make a stew, and he had several dubious bits of stuff to toss in his cauldron. I think the cauldron was a coal scuttle.

It was an immense success. We both knew our lines, and delivered a performance that easily satisfied those members of the family who managed to stay awake. I don't believe I stammered at all, but I know I came out of the experience anxious to be an actor. People clapped and called for more, and I remember the shining smile on Dad's face, the fun and the pleasure. I felt as close to the family as I was supposed to feel because of Christmas. And in my way I had succumbed to the witches and their promise of some sultry, dangerous ambition beng fulfilled.

I was doing well at Rosemead, though I hated it and dodged it. One September when school started again I was pushed ahead by two forms, not one, and so I was with older children. And the school began talking to my mother. They explained that the Education Act allowed for public schools—the grand places esteemed in *Tom Brown's Schooldays* and such—and offered a few places to scholarship boys, promising students who could not otherwise afford the fees. The school closest to us where this was possible was Dulwich College. Were my parents interested in my going there?

Maybe the question was posed by Miss Plumridge, the head of Rosemead, because the school had already detected my dislike of regular attendance. And whereas Rosemead was small and friendly, Dulwich was vast and procedural. It took in two hundred new boys every year, and there would be bullying, et cetera. I had seen a film of *Tom Brown's Schooldays* (where younger boys were roasted in front of an open fire) as well as another picture, *The Guinea Pig*, in which the baby-faced Richard Attenborough pretended to be a boy of humble origins sent to a grand public school, a place called Saintbury (he was twenty-six, but playing half that age!). He was very unhappy there. He was teased and bullied and ragged and humiliated and in general the film made its school look like a prison. But Dulwich was a great opportunity, and Rosemead thought I was able. The talk went on over my head, I suppose. As well it might. In advance, I could not have understood the daunting system in Dulwich or the challenge. But I had to go to school somewhere. It was the law.

I never thought to say to anyone that if education was the person's decision to take responsibility for the task themselves and to follow it through as long as life lasted, then I was settled. I did not like to be taught what to know. I wanted to find it out for myself. I had started to read and was raiding adult-book shelves and library resources to pursue that. With my pocket money I bought paperback books—Penguins. And I was more or less of the opinion

that if you found something in one book you did not
understand then you looked it up in another book. I might
have said—though I'm sure I lacked the wit then—that I
was being taught so much by what things looked like on
film. Of course, many things in film are invented—
designed and made—but even then they represent what
someone thinks. And when it came to a film like *The Third
Man*, there was ruined Vienna—a place I had no chance of
ever seeing, and one that has grown in my mind ever since,
so that one day it became a place where I could find Musil,
Mahler, and Schiele (and the way Schiele, decades in
advance, had guessed the size of the eyes and the look on
the faces in the pictures from concentration camps).

I did as I was told. I worked hard at Rosemead at things
I found too easy like spelling, learning tables, the dates of
kings, places on the map, and so on. (As far as I recall,
"science" did not exist.) The things that made me linger
far longer, and which interested me more, were questions
like, Why does Harry Lime nod at Holly Martins, as if giving Holly permission to shoot him? Are they friends or
enemies?

I read the newspapers and I knew the names of places—
Berlin and Korea, Malaya and India, Palestine and Israel—
where there was trouble, or action, but I had no way of
reconciling the real India with *The Lives of a Bengal
Lancer*. That seemed impossible. I saw a little man in a
white suit and spectacles in a cinema newsreel, pushing his
hand at a camera; it was Harry Truman, and he'd won,
which was a surprise. I saw similar pictures of bombs
exploding, pretty puffball bombs that were just for practice. Twelve twelves were a hundred and forty-four—*i*

before *e*, except after *c*, hence the spelling of deceive. My dad is terrific. My dad is a mystery. Multiple-choice questions are always the hardest.

And then one day at Rosemead, I was called into the teachers' lunchroom. It was a smoke-filled room; maybe they were playing cards—canasta, the game my mum liked? And Miss Plumridge said to me, "You have been accepted at Dulwich. We are all very proud of you." There was another boy in the same class—Roderick Blackburn— who was accepted too. But we weren't friends. Of course, none of the girls were up for Dulwich. It was boys only. And that seemed about as uneducational as anything could be. I came home and told my mum but it turned out she knew already, and I could see that she was worried.

Mum took me on a visit to Dulwich. It was enormous, like a great palace in its own park. It had playing fields that stretched on forever. And the buildings were buildings from old-fashioned adventure films—the school had been founded in 1619. When the boys ended a class, they were like ants scurrying to their next assignment. They wore uniforms: black jackets, long gray trousers. When we went to the school commissariat, we discovered that the white shirts were with separate, detached, and starched collars, and a fresh collar was required every day. You had a front stud and a back stud and cuff links and I wondered if eight years at Dulwich—or whatever the sentence—would be enough to learn how to tie your tie and put on your collar with just human fingers as tools.

"Are you scared?" asked Sally when we got back from the clothes shopping. She was smoking a cigarette. Sometimes it was frightening the way she had grown up.

"I am," I said.

"Hard luck, I can't be there with you," she said. "I'm sorry."

"I can pretend."

"They might not like that."

"What do you mean?"

"Just pretending I'm here." She blew a pretty smoke ring and we watched it shimmy across the space between us.

"Well, you are here—I mean here." I meant at home. But she just looked at me as if wondering when it would all sink in.

"I may not go," I told her.

"Got to go somewere," she said.

"Boys don't talk to you there," I said. I had heard that older boys royally ignored the new bugs.

"You'll make friends," she said. "Bound to. That's what boys do."

"What about girls?"

She thought for a moment and said, "Oh, it doesn't matter with girls." And she paused. "Have you heard the school song?"

"Song?"

"That's right. I've heard some of the boys singing it. On the train. There's a line, '*Detur soli Deo gloria.*' It's Latin—you'll have to learn that—and it means 'Let the glory be to God alone.'" She grinned. "I've heard the boys singing," and she sang herself, soft and low, like Judy Garland singing to Tootie: "*Detur soli Deo gloria*—Herne Hill, Brixton, and Victoria."

She left the strange mix of liturgy and local railways hanging in the air. "You'll have fun with lads like that."

THIRD PART

18

I HAVE ARRANGED THINGS to suggest that Dulwich was a huge break. And so it was. It was like the army—and I was broken, or damaged, or deeply disturbed. Or whatever. But in a way Dulwich simply took advantage of my existing weaknesses. I don't want to blame the school or be unfair to it. As time passed, the school found a way to be very generous to me, and very helpful. And while I never ever got over the dread of the place and the abiding wish not to go, the school gave me the resources I needed to give it up one day. Even now I don't know whether that was the "right" decision. But my education had left me very wary of "right" or correct decisions and much more persuaded by determinations I had made. So Dulwich wrecked me—no doubt about it—but it also made me.

One day in September 1951 I turned up as one of the two hundred new bugs, raw around the collar, and tried to find a place of some security. The scale of it all was overwhelming. At least half of the intake that year were LCC scholarship boys, places traded away for government funds to build a new science block. After all, a great school in the nuclear age had to have a science building. That first day the students were assembled in the school's Music Room to be addressed by Mr. Thomas, the Deputy Master of the school. The Master himself—a man named Gilkes—was unwell.

Thomas was a Welshman; he was small, but a battleship, and very stern. He looked at us and said, in effect, "I see before me the cream of South London. It is just that this year the cream has turned a little sour." Not one of us, I suspect, knew what he meant, or what philosophical splits there might be within the school as the postwar Labour government drew to its close. (The Conservatives, still under Churchill, were returned to power in October 1951, and in my family there was an air of relief at that, as if justice had been done.) But his sarcasm was not to be missed. The lash fell, and Thomas revealed his helpless failure to admit changing times. (Dulwich still exists, but it has reverted to the status of a private, fee-paying school. The experiment of letting gravel in the gold was brief, and I was one of its lucky recipients.)

Before Thomas stood a mongrel group that might start to change England. Consider: if some poor kids went to a toff school, and if some toffs had had to put up with a slum council school. "Daddy, there are boys who are dirty and who know no Latin!" If you wonder where the spirit of such anarchic humor as *The Goon Show* and *Monty Python* came from, don't forget the amazed attitude of some London louts that they had been sucked into the citadel of privilege. Or that they intended to change the antique place. After they'd had their nervous breakdowns.

I can no longer recall the timing or the sequence. Sometimes it occurs to me that anyone looking at films gets into the habit of reordering the timeline: it "works better," don't you think, if we know this before we discover that? So the events that happened become items in a reconstruction. In which case, perhaps that sort of person—a film person—is unusually casual about cause and effect. He or she is ready to see the story. But be careful, for the same ten events may provide different stories depending on their arrangement. I'll go even further: What is an event? It sounds and feels like a tidy, self-contained packet delivered by FedEx. But suppose the "event" is seen more generously or openly as everything and every bit of light that came over the threshhold that day. A new baby is described as a happy event, but any parent knows that the event is a mere marker for an atmosphere and a life that has become so much more complicated.

But if I'm doing my early life as a movie then I want to impress on the screenwriter the need for a crisis. Screenwriters need little encouragement. I can see his or her eyes widening with the discovery. "Got it! Your first day at school, you're in dismay and confusion. There's a class in which the teacher is showing that classic painting, *And When Did You Last See Your Father?* It's a boy being questioned by the Roundheads, I think, and you have to answer, and your stammer suddenly sets in and you can't say a word! How do you like that?"

Do I have to say, "Sm-m-m-m-m-ashing!"?

It didn't happen like that. I cannot even offer a chain of

events in which it happened. I am still not sure what "it" was. The school was intimidating. Many of the teachers wore gowns. There was corporal punishment in class. Prefects could beat boys—thrash them on the bottom with a cane. There were initiation rituals, like the "bumps" for new boys. But the bumps were painless and fun. The thrashings were confined to older boys. The teachers who still smacked were on the decline. And there was a new generation appearing that had heard of "child psychology." Still, Dulwich was a self-conscious public school because it was not in the first rank (Eton, Harrow, Rugby, Winchester) and because some of its greatest defenders were alarmed by the prospect of the cream being sour.

But I do recall that first term that all boys be required to watch the school's First XV in its rugby matches with other schools. The boys were organized by house—there were six houses, and I was in Marlowe—and a roll was called. All I had to do when "Thomson" was shouted out was answer, "Here"—but suddenly I could not. My throat and mouth went into constrictions. I bubbled. I gargled. I stammered. And some boys laughed in a good-natured way. I had stammered before, and at Rosemead, where I was a star, I sometimes made fun of it myself first before anyone else. Perhaps people thought it was an act. It became noticeable. At Dulwich, I asked other boys to answer for me, but the natural disinclination to volunteer for anything made that ruse unpopular. So maybe boys avoided me, for fear of beng asked. In a way, if I hid they were left waiting for my performance. The panic spiraled. And soon I had great difficulty in saying anything at school for four or five years. (There is still a terror that it could come back—or reappear in my children.)

Misfortune seemed to hound me. I found I quite liked rugby, and I was reasonably good at it. But I found myself cast in the role of scrum half, the one person in the game who is obliged to speak. When the scrum half feeds the ball into the scrums (sixteen boys pushing hard against each other), he has to say, "Coming in blues, now!" I could not always say it. Scrums collapsed waiting for me. I was once sent off the field for having engineered such a collapse. I aspired to other positions, silent and tight-lipped, but no, I had scrum-half "material." So the agony went on, though I know at the time I saw the joke, and I experimented with other calls that were easier to say but that sometimes had the scrum slide apart from laughing. The Ministry of Funny Walks and the tactics of absurd command were part of the same comedy of humiliation.

My father did not change much as I grew older, as far as I could see. What did that mean? Looking back on it now, I could see several possibilities. He had had a slight stammer himself as a younger man, and it could reappear. I think the parent is stricken to find a thing like that arising in his children. Whether it happens through association or unwitting imitation or genetically, there must be a load of responsibility. He never disussed it—but of course he hardly ever discussed anything. My graduation to "big school" may have made him uneasy. I think I became more argumentative with him, and he did not appreciate that. But I was learning ideas of a kind that had not crossed his mind. I wonder also whether in his talks with the other woman in his life there had not been some thought that, when I graduated, he might come clean and move more thoroughly away. Well, I can hear her making that case, and I can see him silent but nodding. Equally, my mother

may have said—and I don't know how much she was ever
able to, or allowed to, refer to the other woman—that his
son was under stress. Are you sympathizing with Dad yet,
or do you see his weakness as the source of all the trouble?
I only ask because I still ask myself.

The stress of school was not small. I was being put to
many new tests—French, Latin, higher mathematics—and
I was not getting much chance at things I really liked (making stuff up). In English, we worked on grammar and clause
analysis (things I enjoyed), but not on storytelling or literary appreciation. I was in 1E in the Junior block, led by the
likeable Mr. Booth, and I made friends in a class that
included Smith E. P. (he had a twin brother, C.J.), Thor-
nington, Wadey, Shroff, Perkins, Gilkes (the son of the
Master of the school), Brown, Downes, Hardy, Beevers,
Jenkins, Hall, and Eveleigh.

We were the midgets and the novices in a school that
housed immense men. The cricket pavilion clock had been
stopped, and it was said that this was in honor of Trevor
Bailey, who had been to Dulwich and was by then a leading talent in the English cricket team. Had he really hit the
clock and stopped it? Dulwich was an odd school, founded
in 1619 by Edward Alleyn, one of the top actor-managers
in the age of Shakespeare. School tradition was an important subject. Thus we learned that Sir Hartley Shawcross, a
notable lawyer at the Nuremberg trials, was an old Alleynian, along with a mighty and stirring trio of writers: P. G.
Wodehouse, C. S. Forester (who wrote the Hornblower
books, of which I was very fond), and—how could this
be?—an American writer named Raymond Chandler. If
you read Chandler, it is striking to find that the very cool,

urbane Marlowe—a version of Humphrey Bogart—also has an old-school integrity that is horrified when wanton women throw themselves at him. The Alleynian tradition had extended to several actors, including Leslie Howard and Clive Brook. Yet it says something odd about the school or its focus that in 1951 and the years thereafter no one told me that Michael Powell—of *The Red Shoes*, *A Matter of Life and Death*, and *I Know Where I'm Going*— had been to Dulwich. But, of course, it was a similar deficiency in the school's life that it could not, among several hundred boys, nudge me and say, Look, there is someone for you. Michael Ondaatje came to Dulwich a couple of years after me, and it is a part of our friendship now that we don't believe we ever spoke to each other at school. Of course, he was younger than me, and easy ties did not reach beyond your year. He was also one of that group of pupils ushered into assembly after the C of E religious ceremonies. I don't know why, but Michael was from Ceylon, and I'm sure racism played a part in my attitude, at least.

My first year at Dulwich felt numb. I had already fallen into a deeper pattern of truancy. To get to school I took the 49 bus to Crystal Palace and then changed to the 3. I often got off the 49 around Streatham Common and the Rookery, and walked there before going home. This was a mounting cause of concern. I just about kept up with the schoolwork, but without showing any promise or individuality.

In the Michaelmas term and the first half of Lent, there was rugby. In the second half of Lent was track, and at that I excelled. In the summer on Wednesday and Saturday afternoons the grounds were turned over to cricket. I had seen cricket with Dad at Mitcham and he had bowled to me on the Common. It was only at Dulwich that I realized I had ability. I played a bit for the school's under-twelve side, and I figured for Marlowe. I started playing every evening until about ten o'clock when the summer light faded away.

It was the hard ball that did it. As a little boy I had played with tennis balls, like Henry V, which was sensible. But at Dulwich we used the real thing. Dad gave me one for Christmas, cherry red and shining from deep within, stitched in hard cream stitches that made a seam. Herein lay the ability of the ball to move, off the seam, with spin, or even in the air. But what I loved most was the way the bat trembled in your hands if you really hit and middled the ball. You could feel the tingling, and marvel at the way, if you timed the ball properly, it sped away from your bat. I loved everything about cricket. In the summer of 1951, the South Africans toured Britain and I was taken to see their all-white side (Rowan, McGlew, McLean, Nourse, Endean, Van Ryneveld, Waite, Tayfield, Rowan, McCarthy, Melle) play Surrey at the Oval. We went with my great-uncle Sydney from Prince Rupert when he came over on a visit. I suppose that would have been a bad time for Dad to quit us—with Syd a magical patron! He had me explain cricket to him, and he gave me my first bicycle.

The Oval was intoxicating. There was a brewery nearby, and I loved the yeasty smell in the air. A large ground where the great players came and went was still in Kennington, about a twenty-five-minute bus ride from where we lived. In 1951 Surrey was approaching a period of dominance in the county game that would last for nearly a decade. Having been introduced by Dad, I would go to matches on my own in the summer holidays. I saw a great side: Fishlock, Fletcher, Clark, Constable, May, Eric Bedser, McIntyre, Lock, Laker, Alec Bedser, and Surridge, the skipper of the team and the owner of a cricket gear company. "Surridge" was written on every cricket ball we had.

Every weekend morning Dad and I would go to the Common. We had found a spot where you could play using two trees as wickets. We played liked this: Each side batted for twelve balls. We scored runs on the strength and distance of hits. We gave the bowler points for getting an out or beating the bat. We played with a hard ball and no pads. I think Dad was surprised at my ability. He had nursed me along at every sport since I was a kid. But at cricket I had promise. I bowled quickly enough for him to watch out for his legs. And I could hit his bowling.

One day he hit one of my deliveries very hard. It came straight at me. Too fast for me to duck or get out of the way. I stuck out my hands and caught its roar and its searing smack. I can remember the look of horror on his face, for I think he felt he might have maimed me. Then he shouted out, "Bravo!" It lasted me years.

19

I F YOU'D ASKED ME, "Do you have a dad?" in the early '50s there would have been no doubt. We had been planning to see the film *Ivanhoe* together for some time. We had seen trailers for it and he had known the Walter Scott novel. I had toy figures of Ivanhoe, the Saxon, and Sir Brian de Bois Guilbert, the Norman, though I had only a slight sense then of how Saxon and Norman lay at the root of class differences in Britain. But a few days before the *Ivanhoe* weekend, I broke several bones in my foot playing rugby. In fact, I had carried on playing and was trudging to the bus stop after the game when a teacher saw my limp and sent me back to the school sanatorium. From there an ambulance took me to the hospital. By the time my mother arrived, I was in a plaster cast up to the knee. But it turned out that a medical student had applied the cast and done it wrong. So the next day I went back and a scornful doctor set me right.

But I was not supposed to walk on the plaster for several days, and we had no car. So Dad took one look and carried me on his back to *Ivanhoe*, as if I were the knight and he the horse. It was a boy's adventure, and I believe I told people about it with great pride. It must also have been a labor for him. I was eleven, and the plaster was the weight of another couple of years. But he was strong and made for gestures.

I was the same way. We went on one of our summer holidays to Criccieth, in north Wales. And as was his habit then, he left us—Mum and me—on the first Saturday. He went back and we stayed on together.

At Criccieth, the guest house where we stayed was some way from the railway station. The guest house had a car service that ran people in for a train, and that Saturday morning all three of us made the trip. It was only on the platform that Dad remembered he'd left the picnic lunch the guest house made up for travelers. By then, the car was gone. So I ran back and got it. Say it was a mile each way, and there wasn't much time. But I made it, and no packet of sandwiches was ever delivered with more love or more regret that he wouldn't be there the second week.

In the summer nearly every year for ten years we went a couple of times to Freshwater on the Isle of Wight, to Falmouth in Cornwall, to Lyme Regis in Dorset, to Harrogate in Yorkshire, to Oxford and Cambridge (as a warm-up). Dad always chose the places, and in advance he'd talk like a brochure about where we were going: the castles and the stately homes, the famous walks and so on. Criccieth was the "pearl of the Cambrian coast," even if it rained every day. But it didn't bother me because there was a very nice blond girl at the guest house and we played card games through the overcast.

We never went abroad, but that was a far-fetched venture for our class then, way beyond Dad's intense xeno-phobia and the prevailing currency restrictions. (I have an old passport of my father's parents, with Dad's name attached for a two-week trip to France, in 1923, entering and departing by way of Dieppe. He was fifteen. Did something happen then that made him hate foreign lands?) He thought it wrong (as in unpatriotic) to go abroad, a sign of weakness or disloyalty, and of no practical utility since it meant putting money in alien nation banks. It didn't trouble me too much because the places we went were interesting. We swam in the cold sea. We walked. We saw abbeys and ruins and historical sites. I was taught the outlines of hotel life and he was very funny sometimes in the dining room, watching the other guests and imagining the real inside story about them. (If only he'd told that story about us!) So long as I was a good audience I was all right.

The most important of the summer trips was to Stratford-on-Avon. We did the sites, of course, Anne Hath-away's cottage, Clopton House, and so on. But more important, we went to the Memorial Theater. We had advance tickets for one play, as I remember, and we had to wait in line in the early morning for tickets to two others. We saw *The Merchant of Venice*, with Emlyn Williams as Shylock and Margaret Johnston as Portia; we saw *Love's Labours Lost*, which I have never seen again; and we saw Alan Badel as *Hamlet*.

I was too young to fully grasp *Hamlet* but I'm sure that's what Shakespeare said as it ran through his own head and hands too. I was old enough, however, to register theatrical suspense, the almost insolent antic beauty of

Badel, and the clear apprehension that here was a great work that would never leave you. Today, Badel may not be a familiar name, but in the 1950s, when he was in his early thirties, he was thought to have high promise. He was a chum of Richard Burton's and he had a shot at Hollywood, going there to play John the Baptist in Rita Hayworth's *Salome*—more a side dish than a real chance. For me, he was a great Hamlet—he *was* the part—and he severely tested the conclusion I had reached at school, that I could not do the thing I most wanted to do there, which was to try out for a school play. I did an audition, and I could hardly say a word. It was like expecting to play scrum half with your leg in plaster. Sorry, old chap!

But in the theater at Stratford, I could feel the excitement of being onstage with a great story to tell and Hamlet's father as my Sally. I wanted to be there, and I was hot with regret sometimes. It all worked out very strangely. More than ten years later, by chance, I came to know Badel socially—him, his wife, Yvonne, and their daughter, Sarah. And it was in that later period that Badel put on a production of Jean-Paul Sartre's *Kean*, about the great English actor who died in 1833. It is a very clever, funny play about the overlap of life and stage, and it was perfectly suited to Badel's wit and panache. He was dazzling, though I think it was clear by then that he had missed his moment; a young generation of painfully sincere actors had come along. He was sometimes said to be "difficult." I don't know the details or the truth of it, but he could have had a temper and austere moods that might chill the air. But his brilliance in *Kean* inspired one of the first things I ever wrote, in which Keanery rather invaded Badel's own life. It was a desperate comic dance in which actors lost their own selves. I never dared tell him what he had meant to me, though he had a look so darkened by glory he probably guessed the imprint he had left. He was the first actor I ever knew personally, and he was plainly troubled and bitter beneath all the charm. I could see that a season as Hamlet might sustain or warp a life.

The season at Stratford prompted me to start going to the theater in London. I had been a movie snob, but why restrict myself? As a young teenager I went to see the first London production of *The Iceman Cometh*. It was so long, I think it started at six o'clock in the evening, and the cast included Ian Bannen, Patrick Magee, Michael Bryant, Jack MacGowran, and Lee Montague. I saw Vivien Leigh and Claire Bloom in *Duel of Angels*—I don't know why, except for their starriness. I saw Olivier in *The Entertainer* and in his bloody *Titus Andronicus*, and Ralph Richardson in Robert Bolt's *Flowering Cherry*. I went to see John Neville doing Shakespeare at the Old Vic, with the young Judi Dench when she was a sexpot. I think this was as late as 1959, but I have never seen anything as stunning as Patrick McGoohan in Ibsen's *Brand*, in that intimate theater, the Lyric Hammersmith, where you could see spittle in the air and grab it.

Yet absence—which is acting on the screen—meant the most. I had been pursuing films as best I could. I went all the time, with no more program than what my local theaters chose week by week. I was interested enough to ask at the library whether there were any books on film. One was offered, *The Film and the Public*, by Roger Manvell. I knew his name, in that he was sometimes on *The Critics*, a radio program I loved and trusted. His book was as odd as its title, I thought then. Still, it had lists of films to see and useful commentary on a select band of pictures.

Moreover, you must understand that in 1955 I had no way of seeing "old" pictures. The cinemas showed only new things. We had no television, but that new medium had hardly touched old movies yet. Movies in history were gone, which is one reason why so many are lost forever. But there was one film above all in Manvell's account that attracted my attention: *Citizen Kane*, by Orson Welles.

London in 1955 was a home for Orson. It was there that he took over the Duke of York's Theater and put on an improbable production of *Moby Dick Rehearsed*, his own play about a traveling theatrical company performing the Herman Melville classic. It ran only a few weeks, with a handpicked cast that included Gordon Jackson, Kenneth Williams, Joan Plowright, and Patrick McGoohan. It is famous for all its low-budget intimations of being at sea, or face to face with a great white whale. That same summer, Orson was married (for the third time), to Paola Mori, at Caxton Hall in London.

So he was out and about in London, and that's how, I assume, someone said, "Well, I wonder what *Citizen Kane* would look like now?" It had not been seen for fourteen years. It was famous, but it had been a flop. At any event, in the summer of 1955 I saw in our local paper—the *Streatham News*—that the Classic, Tooting (the nearest we had to a repertory theater), proposed to play *Citizen Kane* for three days. My natural reaction was that a large part of the world had been waiting—like Reg Harris coiled at the top of a bend—for just this moment. So I got to the Classic very early on the first day of the run. It was a nice summer day, and the world was careless. I was the only person there for that first screening.

I might have been deflated at first, but had I been alone for two hours with Grace Kelly—the only thing I can think of that meant as much as this film—I could not have been better treated. To see *Kane* in a theater on your own is the natural way. It brings out the megalomania.

No, I couldn't exactly follow the convoluted narrative. But it must have been a freshly struck print and I knew I had never noticed such emotional texture in a film image before. Later on, I would learn that some people felt *Kane* was too clever or tricky or technical for its own good. For me, it was always a film seeping like a wound in Kane's mind. I felt Kane breathing, sighing—there were wells of sound never attempted before in movies. I loved the man, and I was pained at his solitariness. I knew Welles just a little from *The Third Man* and a few other films (like *The Black Rose*) where he acted, or overacted, but this was clearly him. And this was of his own making and dreaming. I am far from the only movie person who was marked forever by this loss of virginity. But I felt shock at discovering such power, and I wanted to be involved in it somehow.

I told everyone to see the picture.

"Never heard of it," said Sally.

"It's terrific," I said.

"Who's in it?" she asked.

"Orson Welles!"

She smiled. "Oh, him!" she said. "I heard about him." In her very sly, knowing way.

"What did you hear?"

"There, but for the grace of God, goes God," she said.

"What does that mean?"

"I don't know. He looks like you, though."

"Does not!" I said proudly.

"Same baby face," she said. "Could be your dad."

"If you don't stop," I said, exultant, "I'll hit you."

"Well, fuck me!" she said, and there was another of life's mysteries opening up.

20

STAMMERING IS A SILLY little thing. It won't kill you, but it'll change the course of your life. The cures are as many and as helpless as the explanations for it. I am still haunted by the memory of a movie never made in which a group of stammerers come together and employ their "handicap" to rob a great casino. The small and taciturn gang has one female accomplice, a suitably beautiful babe who would sooner do her nails than talk. Her otherwise undetected progress among the guys is marked by the fact that for a half an hour or so after being with her every former stammerer is made as chatty as Oscar Wilde.

One teacher at Dulwich, having observed my efforts to speak, called me aside at the end of a class and addressed me as the Great White Doctor might have done a savage in Africa. "Very aggravating condition, old chap. Fortunately, I picked up the remedy in my own school days." And so he instructed me. At the first hesitation, I was to stamp my foot on the floor where I was sitting. "Just the ticket," he said. Percussion freed the strangled process. It worked—for twenty minutes. I actually bruised my foot on the stone floor of the classroom, but a few words spilled out. Then, after twenty minutes, I had to stamp several times more. By which time the mischievous wits of my classmates had perceived the outline of a rag, and they became an impromptu of orchestral percussions. (Have you seen that Irish show where everyone stamps all the time?) Desks were banged, books dropped, hands clapped together, the odd paper bag was blown up. To cut a romp short, I was finally smacked in the face by the same teacher for having set off a near riot of small explosions. I daresay the teacher involved was now convinced that his own benevolence was wrongheaded when it came to the vermin of these boys.

And he was right. The boys at Dulwich—so many of them newcomers to privilege, or unaccustomed to intellectual devotion—responded to the school with all manner of plans for ragging the teacher. It seemed to be the one thing we had learned in primary school. There were tyrants—a Mr. Treadgold, for instance, genuinely feared throughout the school for his cruelty when keeping order. There were also good blokes who enjoyed some fun and reckoned to be honest fellows but still the boss. Then there were teachers whose academic brilliance was daily shadowed by incompetence in the matter of controlling twenty-five boys with insurrection in mind. There was one teacher, a gentle soul—I will not name him—whom I saw reduced to tears by one class. Goaded and tortured, at the crisis of crises he declared that he was going to report us to the Master. So he stormed out of the room and slammed the door. The class then passed the time of day for fifteen minutes or so, whereupon one daredevil opened the door and enquired of the cowering teacher, "Wouldn't you like to come back in, sir?" It was a formal requirement—and not just malice— that boys always addressed teachers as "sir."

In the middle-age levels of the school, this disorder was common enough and so some violence was permitted to teachers. Moreover, ironic sarcasm was a feature of the school, so there were some teachers who believed my stammer was just a ploy to catch the gullible and softhearted. Gradually, teachers ignored me. They did not call upon me to stand up and continue translation of Caesar's *Gallic Wars,* or to list the industries of India. That may have been meanness to me, as well as a way to quell pandemonium or worse—and there were other cures suggested.

The most terrible of these came from the Master of the school himself—Gilkes, if you remember. In my second year he returned from illness and taught a class that was called "Scripture." This turned into Bible reading, at which I slowed the class's progress and could make a miracle seem dragged out and laborious. Mr. Gilkes rose to the challenge. The answer he had was very simple: I was to sing the words, and then, he said, "Surprisingly, you will find that you have no trouble at all."

I sighed. Like everyone at the school, I had auditioned for the choir—a notable institution—and been rejected as "a church with just one bell." Couldn't sing. Mr. Gilkes would have none of it, and I was charged to carry on in the latest doings of Moses in what was still a bold treble voice. I was hushed, so the rest of the class laughed silently.

Gilkes protested. A social experiment was conducted. And when I sang I could read. Gilkes beamed in vindication. Very soon, in geometry or whatever, a wiseacre voice would suggest, "'E could sing it, sir. Really, a very sweet voice."

This was a sign, of course, to the other boys—many of whom were official choristers—to break into alternative or descant versions of my limited song. Tremulous monkeys of choral work were soon swinging in the air. Chaos is come again. (And who was most obviously available as the ringleader, if not instigator?)

However, I was modestly impressed. The singing did work, even if it was not yet possible to imagine myself in a Jacques Demy–Michel Legrand picture, singing, "Pass the salt . . . Thanks . . . You're so pretty." So I took singing home at night to the bathroom and experimented. The "song" may have been unrecognizable to others, but I was fluent, and I began to look for voices and lyrics that were more beguiling than the Moses story or the proofs of theorems. So began my relationship with Frank Sinatra.

My mum helped. She loved Sinatra and was often listening to him on the radio. Moreover, my mum could sing and sometimes she joined in with Frank. I had seen Frank in *From Here to Eternity* (a major event in my life), and then in two other films, *Suddenly* and *Young at Heart*. I was riveted. In *Young at Heart* he was a sad songwriter who didn't really want to live (unless he could have Doris Day). In one scene he is driving in the snow and turns off the windshield wipers—as if to say, It's a gamble. I thought this was immensely cool—but not half as arresting as seeing Frank as a gunman in *Suddenly* who means to shoot the president.

Shoot the president! I thought, That's pretty nasty.
(Never doubt the quality of timing, for Frank's role in my
story hangs on the arrival of long-playing records and the
mood for shooting presidents.)

Frank made his first long-playing album, *Swing Easy!*,
in 1953. And then in 1954, 1955, and 1956, he came out
with *Songs for Young Lovers, In the Wee Small Hours,* and
Songs for Swingin' Lovers. It seemed marvelous to me that
so vivid an actor could sing so well and know such songs. I
only noticed songs with Frank. Indeed, I think I went
straight from nursery rhymes to "My Funny Valentine," "I
Get Along Without You Very Well," and "I've Got You
Under My Skin."

I was given a record player for the Sinatra albums and I
played them all the time, doing Frank as I listened to them,
holding a hairbrush as a microphone. I could not sing, but
I could mime, and I was thrilled at the dream that the
words were passing through me with the rhythm and the
pacing and the sad magic of knowledge that Frank possessed—or was possessed by.

A great event in this passion was a film called *High
Society.* I had been told that it was a remake of *The
Philadelphia Story* with Frank in the James Stewart part.
But it also promised Grace Kelly (a steady infatuation) in
what was her last job before the insane Monaco gig. (She's
going to regret it, I told the world.) Bing Crosby was there
too, and my mum engaged me in friendly arguments about
whether Bing was a better singer than Frank. And there
was Louis Armstrong, not for the first time. Two years
before *High Society,* I had seen *The Glenn Miller Story.* In
truth, I had seen it many times, because I cried and cried to

it from love of the Miller music, which already had the glow of nostalgia to it. I was soft on Jimmy Stewart and the idea of Miller never being found, and I was entranced by a scene where Glenn learned how to arrange and play a tune to get his sound right. So the audience felt itself participating. There was also a moment when Glenn and his boys went to a basement club to see and hear Louis Armstrong. And it was as if Louis were the source of Glenn's music, albeit at a subterranean level.

The following year, 1955, there was a similar film on Benny Goodman. It was not as good a film, but still I loved the way Goodman played his clarinet. That's "jazz," said an older boy I was friendly with. "Is that like Frank Sinatra?" I asked. "Why not?" he replied. "Frank's a cool singer."

And so, almost exactly as rock and roll was beginning, with all the great damage that could do to music and other things, I had the huge good luck of discovering jazz (and I'm really not sure how easily anyone can do that anymore). A friend with a guitar was trying to play a song called "Rock Island Line" that had just been recorded as "skiffle" by a man named Lonnie Donegan, who was also the banjo player in Chris Barber's Jazz Band. (I saw him play live once, with Chris's wife, the singer Ottilie Patterson.)

This was known as traditional or New Orleans jazz. There was another band—that of Ken Colyer—purer than the Barber band. And there was a suave, heroic figure, Humphrey Lyttelton (who died in 2008). He was Eton and the Guards and very wellborn, I heard, but he had that lazy-elegant English voice that might be American. It was correct but cool and reminded me of Alistair Cooke. Humph was also involved in a newspaper cartoon, *Flook*, in the *Daily Mail*, drawn by another musician, Wally Fawkes. Humph would talk about what anyone in jazz owed to Armstrong as if he had made the world listen.

I became a record collector at the Swing Shop in Streatham and at Dobell's on the Charing Cross Road. I was given Armstrong's Hot Seven recordings for Christmas and was transformed by the soaring trumpet solos. In the space of a year I rescued myself from the monotony of "traditional" jazz, and first heard the racing downhill of Charlie Parker. I knew he was dead already, skiing in heroin, but Miles Davis had a series of departures: *Birth of the Cool*, *Miles Ahead*, *Sketches of Spain*, *Porgy and Bess*, *Milestones*, *Kind of Blue*.

There were a few boys at Dulwich who led me to jazz. Again, the moment was friendly. The musicians union in Britain had forbidden tours by Americans since the end of the war. But in the mid-1950s its policies were relaxed, and the great figures began to tour. There was a New Orleans veteran, George Lewis. There was a band led by the Dixieland guitarist Eddie Condon. And then it began in earnest: Louis Armstrong and the All Stars; Jazz at the Philharmonic, arranged by Norman Granz; the Modern Jazz Quartet; the Basie Band; the Ellington Orchestra; Thelonious Monk; Miles Davis.

I don't know what these groups thought of England (which was not very black or cool), because they played in strange places like old cinemas and variety halls. Miles Davis came on, squeezed out one bitter blue number, turned his back on the audience, and never played another note. Monk prowled round a dishonest piano. The MJQ seemed to be in a Stockholm chamber designed by Ingmar Bergman. Basie and Ellington blew the roofs off their halls and carried themselves like professional crowd-pleasers. Basie offered the sheer engine of his beat and the Duke teased us royally when he started to open up the old Ellington repertoire only to discover that kid Brits had the records. "Oh," he said after something black and tan. "Oh, you *know* that? Well, we love you madly." And that camp announcement was delicious in an age when we were all trying to tell someone "I love you" for real.

Armstrong was the huge draw. As I recall, his South London concert was at the biggest venue available, the Davis Theater in Croydon. He had that all-star lineup with him—Trummy Young, Ed Hall, Billy Kyle, Arvell Shaw, Barrett Deems—and a singer, Velma Middleton. Louis then was past his best, so he was just intoxicating. He fronted the band in his fond and rascally way, but two or three times a night he would take off on a solo that was so shattering and pure that you knew how in 1927 this guy had had Stravinsky, Goodman, Scott Fitzgerald, and every white woman who heard him ready for the jungle. You could still hear the outrage.

After the show came out, a friend and I hung around. We saw people going to a side door. We followed. And that's how we met him. He was in the doorway in a white shirt and black pants. He was sweating immensely, and he carried a large white handkerchief, the size of a hotel towel, to mop himself. You could feel his heat from several steps away. He made sweating feel divine. And he reached out to touch us white kids, like waifs near his fire. "Thank

you very much for coming," he said, and his hands were
like leather. Years later, it happened that I researched Louis
Armstrong. He was the son of a teenage whore born and
raised on earth floors. He had hardly any education. But
he would play music as intricate and daring as (and more
emotional than) anything in his time. How can such a man
be? He ignores and eliminates education. You can use
every device of history to describe him, but nothing
explains the shock. Some necessary force was delivered.
Some demonstration for the world. Did God send him?
And I daresay at the very same time there were other cities
and other parts of the U.S. where there were dogs and
high-power hoses to counter that force.

Jazz didn't free my speech—it just brought me delight.
And while I was pretending to be Sinatra, I was also making myself available for what I called the American
rhythms in that conversation I quoted ealier—the girl with
the toothache and the newspaper owner. The language was
English, yet the attitudes in the talk—the doubts and
hopes—were something else. ("We love you madly!")
Equally, the seeping romanticism of Frank's songs, so
much at odds with the cynicism of his face, was an American struggle. There were long melodic lines in his songs
(where he, indeed, learned breathing), and meandering
thoughts in the wisteria sentences in Faulkner, in Thomas
Wolfe, and even in Henry James. There was an American
sentence tough and loose enough for you to find out how
little you knew. Whereas the syntax of English English was
often so terse, so definitive, so marked as to be the skeleton
of what you knew. So it felt natural to me that America
had created this music where a striding beat remained in

place as instrumentalists "improvised" for minutes at a time.

The whole thing was beyond me—the nature of flow and where it came from, the quality and pacing of voice in an instrumental music. And then I heard Annie Ross—the sublime, radiant, nimble Ross—who sang musical lines like Wardell Gray out of Kafka: "My analyst told me, I was right out of head / My analyst told me, I'd be better dead." And oh, my brethren, this babe had been born in Mitcham! I believed that it was my way out of silence, even if I wasn't there yet, and still reckoned that I would die if I couldn't speak. I found a record (a Norman Granz production of J. J. Johnson and Stan Getz at the Opera House in Chicago). I played it until the grooves wore away. It was two voices—on trombone and tenor sax—talking to each other. I thought Getz was a genius. (I had a live record from 1950 in which he was introduced as "the Montgomery Clift of the tenor sax.") The time would come, in the 1980s in a club in Oakland, California, when I would see and hear Getz play live. He was not far from his death, and I think he was ill, but he had that quality that musicians can reach, of seeming to stop time for half an hour.

I think when you write prose you need access to a lot of voices and measures, but I know in my head that I sometimes come to sections of a book that need to be like Getz.

"Have you got my Sinatra album, then?" asked Sally.

"It's mine," I said.

"Bloody likely," she told me. "I need it."

"What for?"

"Fellow I know, I want to play it to him."

"I bet he doesn't get it."

"Oh, I think he does," she said in that lazy way.

"What does that mean?" I wanted to know.

"Look at you," she said.

"What do you mean, look at me?"

"Have you ever thought about your Frank?" she asked.

"How?" I said.

"How he's so relaxed, so dreamy. What do you call it?"

"He listens to the words," I told her. "He's an actor."

Sally pursed her lips, stole the album, and gave me a grin. "And he gets laid four or five times a day," she said.

2 I

I PLAYED CRICKET WITH BRYAN, the boy who
lived over the road. We did most things together: we
went cycling into the Surrey hills; we camped; we
hitchhiked once to the Isle of Wight and got there in time
for lunch! At six o'clock in the morning, I would cross the
street and tap on his bedroom window. He'd get up and
we'd go to the open-air swimming bath on Tooting Bec
Common. It was a hundred yards long, a huge place, with
the trains rattling behind the changing rooms. Sometimes
that pool was packed with kids, and it was a girl-watching
mecca as bathing-suit design and puberty struggled to find
confidence after the war.

And we played cricket. One day the bus stopped as
usual quite close to where we played and a black man got
off. I have to put it that way because for us kids it was far
and away the most striking thing about him. He watched
us play hard ball, with no pads for a while. He came a little
closer and fielded the odd ball and tossed it back to us with

the grin that waits to be asked to join in. All fair enough—
we'd done it ourselves. But he was adult and he was black
and we had been told that you didn't just speak to anyone—not on Tooting Bec Common, a resort of prostitutes
and a haven for escaping dictators.

But Ben would not let us be standoffish. He was thin
and wiry. His hair was receding. He was not quite as young
as I had thought at first.

"That looks like a nice bat," he said to me.

I was proud of it. It was a Gradidge and I had taken
care of it, oiling it with lubricious fondness. Linseed oil is
not everyone's taste, but it's a turn-on for some of us, along
with the special staleness of old jockstraps.

I showed Ben the bat. He told us his name. He was from
Barbados.

"Like Everton Weekes," I said, referring to the batsman
who had figured so bravely in the 1950 tour by West
Indies.

"Right you are," he said. "Mind if I have a knock?"

We were on the brink of something. I don't know who
he was. There wasn't a Ben from Barbados who played
seriously. But he was a natural. Bryan and I could both
bowl well enough, and he handled us, remarking on a
really good delivery and whipping the others about the
Common. He was very quick on his feet and in the wrists.
And as he got used to us and the pitch he was something to
see. Then he bowled to us and I suspect he went easy but
you could hear the ball hissing in the air. There was a summer of Ben, getting off the 49 bus at the same time most
evenings. Then he never came back. I don't know what he
was doing in London, unless God had sent him to give us

some lessons. We adored him, and looked out for him for years afterwards, and he was the first black man we ever knew to talk to and be inspired by. Him and Miles Davis, yet this Ben was a prince, and Miles the prince of darkness.

But Ben taught us strokeplay, short-pitched bowling, and how great the game was. And the years took on a rhythm I can still recall: in 1950, West Indies toured England in the summer and won the Test at Lord's, and on the last day their fans started singing calypso at the game and introduced the world to Weekes, Worrell, and Walcott and "those little pals of mine, Ramadhin and Valentine." In 1951, it was the South Africans and the first game I ever saw. In 1952, Fred Trueman scattered the Indian team. In '53, England won back the Ashes (with Compton and Edrich batting), which Australia had held since 1933. I heard the final overs on a radio on the beach at Freshwater. In 1954 came Pakistan with Hanif Mohammad and Fazal Mahmood. In 1955 it was South Africa again.

It was in 1953 that I saw my first day of Test cricket—England vs. Australia at Lord's. A friend and I queued for hours outside the ground and then we sat on the grass just beyond the boundary rope. According to *Wisden*, that 1953 series still holds the British record—more than 500,000—for the most people attending the matches. The day we were there we saw Hutton score a century backed by Graveney against Lindwall and Miller, but by the end of the match, after Australian centuries from Hassett and Miller, Willie Watson and Trevor Bailey had to make a heroic stand for England against defeat.

I was playing cricket at school and was good enough to play on school teams sometimes. I watched the Surrey team assemble. From 1952 until 1958, seven times in a row, Surrey won the County Championship. This was the game I watched. Test matches were expensive and sometimes by ticket only, but the county game was within reach in those days, like the league in soccer. It was the heart of the game, and even Test players strove to be available for county games if they could. There were large crowds and strong feeling if rivals like Middlesex or Yorkshire were playing. Alas, that game is in tatters today. I understand that cricket now is Test cricket—international games—or one-day matches in which both sides have a set number of overs. Is it incidental that the parts of Tooting Bec Common where we played every day until it was dark are overgrown now and past caring?

I doubt a kid in Barbados needed the game more than I did. With the Surrey team I could share in their glory and their suntanned character. As if I were doing Sinatra, I could imitate them all, physically.

I could be the upright Peter May—Charterhouse and Cambridge and England's captain—stroking a drive through the covers. I could be Alec Bedser—the great, gentle Alec—who sustained England against Australia for so long, with a run-up of just a few strides and the greatest medium-pace bowling there ever was. When the air at the Oval was thick and yeasty from the brewery, Alec could move the ball a foot in the air. A foot? You had to be there.

Then there was Jim Laker, the Yorkshire-born off-spinner with just a few stuttery steps and then the arm wheeling over. And Tony Lock, the greatest catcher of a ball, the fiercest competitor, with a left-arm delivery that came and went in a blur—and a good thing, too, for some said he threw the ball when he got worked up. And Bernie Constable, a fine middle-order batsman and a swift cover fielder whose every step on the field was taken with pigeon pride and joy, and whose remarks could have all the close fielders laughing as the bowler ran in.

England was as strong as Surrey in those years, so it felt vital to be at the heart of the game. And the rivalry with Australia was the big brass ring. As I said, we beat them in England in 1953 with Bedser leading the way. But then in 1954–55, we toured Australia, under May's leadership. We had Lock and Laker in their prime. We had Bedser fading away, but with two new bowlers—Brian Statham and a real newcomer, Frank Tyson, who proved to be unplayably fast. Together, they won the series. And Fred Trueman was not even picked for that tour, despite 130-odd wickets in the preceding season. He was "unruly" and "outspoken"—not always an MCC man. Cricket then was a sport ruled by class, and the MCC was a place where the system believed in amateur, university chaps as fit to be skippers. There was even an annual match, the Gentlemen against the Players, where the Players were professionals known by their surnames and the Gentlemen were amateurs, called Mr. Dewes and Mr. Doggart.

The next visit by Australia was 1956. The Australian team was in transition: it had veteran players like Ray Lindwall, Keith Miller, and Neil Harvey, and some kids, great players for the future, Richie Benaud and Alan Davidson. They were led by Ian Johnson, their off-spin bowler, not a strong captain. Quite early on in the season, the Aussies came to the Oval to play Surrey, and in one innings Jim Laker got all ten of them out: 10 for 88. It was a dry summer. The wickets tended to break up. There were Australian complaints that English groundsmen were catering to Laker's rare ability with pitches that did not last a game. I'm sure there was truth in these comments.

England was dominant in the series, but by the time of the fourth Test at Old Trafford in Manchester, the summer was a roaster and the ground was cracking. Laker was a great bowler in his prime and the England team was full of greedy close catchers who would snatch the ball right off the maker's name on the bat. In that Test, Laker took nineteen of the twenty wickets to fall. Nineteen for ninety.

I was in heaven for him, for English cricket, and for my tour de force impersonation of the modest Laker licking his spinning finger and kicking absentmindedly at the dusty pitch. Kids asked me to do Laker.

Bryan and I had met some other cricketers on the Common. Cycling one Sunday afternoon we found a game in progress, the parents having a picnic as a few boys played. The game belonged to a merry boy named Rupert, handsome and a good bat. We dropped our bikes and watched long enough to get an invitation. Long enough for me to see that one of the boys was a girl, a pale blonde with sharp eyes, grey green, and the beginnings of a figure. I ended that blissful Sunday trying to teach her to bowl like Laker. This meant standing close to her and putting her arms in the correct position. I had never been as close to a girl, and so you begin to see the profound benefits of cricket. She giggled and said she'd never get it. But she seemed prepared to try until dusk set in. Her name was Margaret.

22

MY GRANDFATHER, BERT, in Mitcham was seriously ill. He had always had a cough but it grew worse and then it turned out that he had cancer. He had to have an operation that removed his voice box. When he came out of the hospital he had a hole in the front of his neck and a breathing tube. His voice, soft and lulling, was gone. The very best he could do was whisper. This in a story about the difficulty of speaking.

Try as I might, I could not hear or understand what he was saying. I know that I felt this obstacle between us was a version of my stammer. I saw the two things as being alike and I could hardly be with Bert without breaking into tears. He smiled in his charming way and held my hand, but Mum told me not to let him see me upset. So we played cards together—cribbage—and we chuckled silently at the twists of the game. I felt myself understanding him better. With so many people in my childhood, the best way of getting to know them was to find a shared game.

Grandma was always telling me what a problem Bert had been in her life. Sometimes she said this in front of him, and he nodded in his wise way and smiled patiently, as if he'd learned long ago (two world wars ago) to let her temper run on. But I noticed that they liked to sit together in the same simple silence, sipping tea perhaps or doing nothing except be together. They got a television, one of the first I ever saw, and liked to watch the horse racing in the afternoon, as they had gone to the races together for most of their life. Sometimes Grandma would phone the local bookie and they'd put two shillings on a horse they liked the look of, and I think they were always a little ahead of the game, which suggests that horses do photograph as well as people.

On Sunday mornings, Dad and I would go to Mitcham to see Grandma and Bert. Then the bus back and we were in the kitchen. Dad would shout, "Serve the meal!" He became agitated as he grew older if he could smell food but not eat immediately. And my mum would be cooking and listening to the radio—the swooning theme song of *Two-Way Family Favourites*, "With a Song in My Heart," broadcast from London and Hamburg, because even in the 1950s Britain had thousands of troops stationed in Germany.

Often at lunch, there'd be an argument. Dad would lay down the law about something and I would explain to him that he was wrong—I must have been learning something at school. And he would think that there was an edge of hostility creeping into my voice. And he may have been right. So the mood shifted. We were all right together until I began to oppose him, and the more I could command evidence and logic in the case the more surely he seemed betrayed.

And then one Sunday, it started to get dark.

"There's a storm coming," said Mum.

"It's the end of the world," said Dad.

We waited for thunder and lightning, but none came. In about a half an hour, it had gone from bright day to night, except it wasn't even regular night with moonlight. It was thick black fog, and you could smell it.

"They've let off one of those bombs," guessed Dad. "Where's my gas mask?"

There was plenty of talk of bombs at the time. We had hydrogen bombs being tested in the atmosphere and if you read the papers it seemed likely that it was more than the atmosphere could take. The Campaign for Nuclear Disarmament was a kind of duffle-coat hiking club. In a couple of hours, the darkness receded and it went back to being an ordinary, dismal afternoon. The next day in the papers came the report: apparently there had been a very unusual weather system. A great cloud of smog had gathered over London. A breeze took it off, but then the breeze dropped and a freak vacuum had sucked the sooty air back into London at ground level. I was never persuaded. But it led to new laws about smokeless fuels and the attempt to free London from industrial grime.

"It couldn't happen like that," I said.

"Oh, Mr. Know-all says it couldn't have been. That's what we send him to school for, to know more than the experts."

"Did you ever see smog that black?" I asked.

No answer.

"And how did it get sucked back into the city?"

No answer.

"Ooh, Mother," said Dad, "I'm frightened. Mr. Know-all says it's the end of the world."

"No, you said that," said Mum.

"Well," he said, "if I'm going to be contradicted in my own home, I'm off."

"It's not your home," I said, and he swung a blow at me, a smack with an open hand. It missed, and it suddenly seemed that he might be drunk. "I am going to my room," he said. "I know when I'm not wanted."

But did he? Did he have any idea? Downstairs in the house, Grannie's health was faltering. I don't know what it was, or whether it was really anything to die from. But most of my life I had gone downstairs in the morning, to get her newspaper and ours off the front step. And I had always called out, "Good morning, Grannie," as I passed her bedroom, dropping her paper at her door, and there had been some response. Until it stopped. She wasn't dead, but maybe she was sleeping differently. "Too sorry for herself," Mum said.

Some mornings, when I had her paper, Grannie neither stirred nor responded. I have a dream still of creeping past her door, wondering if she is dead. I was fast and nimble then and I could do the stairs and the hall without a sound. I still get the paper, but it's the *New York Times* now, not the *Daily Mail*, and I am not nearly as nimble. I could fall on the steps where the paper deliverer tosses the *Times*, and I wonder whether I'll go before newspapers stop such things as deliveries and newsprint.

Did Grannie die because she was sorry for herself? No

doctor had any other cause until the last moment and then it was pneumonia, but there was something in the family, I think, that would just as soon die.

I learned later that Grannie had told my mother she couldn't climb the stairs anymore. So she couldn't go to the bathroom. But she used a chamber pot that perhaps Mum could deal with. So with Dad away, Mum was getting trapped into being a nurse to his mother. She didn't like it. Mum would say, "She's a dirty old woman." And then it turned out that Dad had done a deal: he had had Grannie give him the house and in return he had promised to provide for her as long as she lived. With Mum doing most of the providing.

Grannie was the first person I knew who died. She was a large presence in my early years. In the passport that she and her husband, Alexander, took out in 1923, their two photographs look out at me. I never knew him, of course, but the facts are there: he was born on June 4, 1877, she on October 27, 1880; he was five foot six, she was five foot five; his eyes were gray, his hair fair, her hair black and her eyes brown. He was a bacon tester, the passport says, and I believe he went around southern England doing just that. And the two of them had a theatrical company. They are gone, and not much more remains than the passport. Lives are so central, so full and eager, so long as someone is trying. Then they collapse. Britain, I learned as a boy, lost nearly half a million people in the war, and the world may have lost fifty million lives. Losing things is so easy. But in the passport, my grandfather's signature is so close to mine. And the more I look at his picture the more I like him.

Some of the mystery of my life began to break down as Grannie died. Mum became very angry and it was now that she told me that Dad was living somewhere else as well as with us. Of course, I'd suspected as much, but I'd been kind to myself by remaining in technical doubt over it. Now I saw that it was a battleground. And the house was a big part of it, because Grannie had once had a will that stated the house was to go to me when she died. All of a sudden, I could see how Mum had tried, and she had done it for me. But my father had changed the rules of the game. The will had been altered as he paid for his mother's upkeep.

He had a car that came with his job. He was now company secretary to the Empire Rubber Company in Luton. So he arrives in a car one Friday just like that. And one day, instead of going to Mitcham on the Sunday, he reckons to drive somewhere else. I went along. I don't know where, but somewhere west of London. And he stops at a pub and lo and behold there are people he knows there. And they are very friendly and eager to meet me. They seem like nice people, but he pretends it's just a chance meeting. When it's over, he drives us home.

"Who were those people?" I ask.

"I don't really know," he says.

"They were acting like old friends!"

"I can't help that."

It was another fight, and over Sunday lunch not a word was said. "We met some old friends," I told Mum.

"We did not," Dad said. He had a way of completely ignoring factual situations.

"Do I know them?" asked Mum.

"No," he said.

"But you knew them," I said.

"I was just being polite," he said.

"No," I said, "you're unbelievably rude, because you lie all the time."

And he got up and went to his room. Never a word of explanation.

I don't mean to put all these events together like a string of beads. They happened over a few years, between my being thirteen and sixteen, let's say, a period in which I could talk to him more and more forcefully.

"Do you see?" Mum said to me once. "You can talk to him."

"What?"

"When you get angry with him you don't stammer. It's a good sign. You'll be free of it one day."

I had hardly noticed this, but it was true. So, when I could get a sentence out, I was ignored. One Saturday, my father and I had been to see Chelsea—it might have been in 1955, the year they won the League—and we were walking back to the South Kensington station to get the bus home. As we were walking, I was talking. And I don't know what I was saying. But at the bus stop as we were waiting for the bus—and there were other people in the line—he suddenly punched me very hard in the stomach. I was completely winded and I was on the ground. He left me there and didn't offer a hand when the bus came. He said nothing about why he had done it, nor about being sorry. To this day I don't know why he hit me, or what had come over him. It was like a mad action.

We got home and Mum could see that something was wrong.

"What happened?" she said.

"Absolutely nothing," he said.

He was soon in his room.

I told her, but I was ashamed at being made so helpless.

It seemed to me he was drinking more. He had always drunk beer but now he was drinking whisky, too. There wasn't any hint of an explanation about it, but this was a man who never spoke about his inner life. I hope as you've read this you've been in no doubt about a certain love he had for me. But in never telling me he loved me, it was like he just did not permit himself that kind of language or that way of thinking. And I never heard he had told anyone else he loved them either.

Sometimes, when he was driving, it was clear he should not have been. We never heard of any trouble—but there was so much we never heard about. After Grannie died, nothing was done with the downstairs flat. It remained the same as ever, with all her clothes and her furniture. But now it was cold and damp and more likely to be haunted. I didn't see that Dad was touched or disturbed. His behavior backed up what Mum told me—that he and his mother had never got on. He had hated her, it seemed, because when he was a boy she had dressed him as a girl and let his hair grow long so that it curled. But the house became his. He said he was thinking of separating the ground-floor flat and renting it out.

On Sunday evenings, we got into the habit of going across the road to Bryan's parents' house for drinks and sandwiches. And it was there that I noticed him drinking more and becoming more difficult if he got into an argument he could not back up.

We came home from one of those evenings and there was a fight—I mean a real physical fight for my life. He attacked me, and in the end I was holding him down on the bed. He was strong and it was all I could do to hold him. I wondered what I would do if he managed to throw me off. But I was bigger than he was by then, and he had drunk too much. He roared at me and said he hated me. He shouted, "Murder!" And then he passed into a drunken sleep.

The next time I saw him it was as if nothing had happened. And really then there was no alternative to the principle of his phantom existence—you could trust nothing.

23

I WAS DOING BADLY at school. I wanted to specialize in history, but that option did not begin until the fifth year, whereas other special tracks started in the third. So I found myself in the lower classes kept for the boys who might collect some O-level passes in the big exams but who were hardly judged material for Oxford or Cambridge. Dulwich was ruthless about this high aim. It measured itself by the number of people it placed every year in "Oxbridge," not by those students who had done good work in suspect areas (I suppose that was why Michael Powell was not referred to) or had overcome significant handicaps.

My school report admitted bleakly that my "lack of participation" was holding me back. But no one ever discussed the reason for that, and the school never called my parents in to talk about it. It was held at arm's length. But I had eliminated so much from my program at the school: doing drama; taking a part in class talks; having as many friends as I wanted; or even turning up for school.

Then one day I had to have my annual "medical" examination at school. It was a strange formality, yet seemingly it was compulsory. Once in every year a student had to go to the medical office and be inspected. Was it a final-resort effort to keep such things as infection and lice out of the school? Was it a tacit acknowledgment that boys from poor homes—the sour cream—might have lacked proper care? This was outrageous and unlikely. After Suez, in the late 1950s, Harold Macmillan would become prime minister, and soon he would be telling Britain, more or less accurately, that "you've never had it so good." But Super-Mac's attitude was rather grudging (did we actually deserve it?), and that went hand in hand with the tight-lipped benevolence that said it was best to check on children's health. I don't know why I'm laughing, because a weird rescue was coming, and again it was a stroke of benevolence from the system that I was lucky enough to receive.

The doctor and the nurse sat me down after the regular physical inspection, and the doctor said, "Now, old chap." I was terrified. Had he spotted tuberculosis or lurgi, the dread disease from *The Goon Show?*

"Spot of trouble talking?" he said.

I nodded. He nodded.

"See what we can do. Letter for your parents very soon."

Within days the letter came and in it the doctor said he felt that I might benefit from speech-therapy classes. These had just been initiated by the London County Council—oh, blessed LCC—and were entirely free. Because they occurred during school hours, the school gave me official permission to be absent. I should attend at an address in

Blackfriars on Saturday mornings (Saturday was normally a school day, with school in the morning and games in the afternoon).

I was not alone. There was another boy in the school, Steve Spooner, younger than me but just as afflicted. We would go together.

That first Saturday, I took the bus to Blackfriars and found the place, just south of the river, not too far from where the National Theater stands now. A woman talked to us. She was friendly, calm. I liked and trusted her from the outset, and she said she was a speech therapist. However, she said, I must not think that stammering was scientifically understood, or even curable. Sometimes it passed. Sometimes it was forever. (One of the best talkers I ever met was Budd Schulberg, and he stammered all the time.) All she could offer was help in a variety of forms.

She told us we had lost the habit of natural breathing because we were in such a state of tension over speaking. Speech, she said, was natural, and needed ease. We began classes on physical relaxation, and she taught us to see how tense we were. So we lay down and gradually and consciously relaxed every part of our body as best we could. We were to practice this technique every day at home. I still do it. And there were breathing exercises in which we enlarged our lungs and began to count and measure how much air we had.

Next we were recorded and asked to make an analysis of our stammer. Nearly every victim has certain sounds and plosive consonants that are unusually challenging. Perhaps they could be avoided—if "Please" was vulnerable, for instance, you could say "May I." You find a different speech formula, and soon realize that vowel sounds are easier openers than most hard consonants. Thus I started to write, or to play with words. For I had noticed some patterns already and had tried to scheme ways around them. But now I had official permission for that, and for the first time I began to see the prospect of a rhythm—a cadence to help me speak—in the way I chose words. I found that I had a brain that could work these things out very quickly. The teacher remarked on it.

Then we isolated the sounds that were still difficult and worked out "sliding" procedures. Very quickly on the brink of such a word, the speaker was to inhale deeply and slow the speech pattern. It worked a lot of the time. Listening to the radio with fresh curiosity I heard others who were doing it already.

Our last test was to go out in the Blackfriars area and say absurd things. I have referred to *Monty Python* before, but the show was still years away and I can only tell you that when it arrived I knew its spirit already from what I called our Saturday-morning "silly set-ups." I was charged, for instance, to go down to the Cut street market, wait in line at a stall clearly selling fruit and vegetables, and say, "Excuse me, do you have any piano strings?"

"What did 'e say?"

"He said have you got piano strings?"

"Does it look like it? What are these, mate? Are they apples, plums, cherries? Or do they look like bleeding piano strings?"

"Ah. Well, then, do you by any chance have some cheese?"

The speech-therapy establishment was new in the area.

Before very long, the word got around that crazy kids with speech defects were likely to be roaming around asking bloody nonsensical questions. So we were treated with a little more tolerance or humor. We were "comedians." We were local novelties, like blind children or newcomers from Jamaica. The object of the exercise was to separate the articulation of speech from its emotional need. I can hear Olivier pouncing on this: "Aha, the Gielgud method!" (And, of course, Olivier knew the Cut, located as it was between the Old Vic and the National.) For others this unusual play had fascinating links to the whole style and content argument. It did encourage mannerism and surrealism, and I'm not being flippant when I talk of *Monty Python*, for the process quite quickly gave me a surrealist view of many everyday English transactions. You might get your head knocked off, but I found something unexpectedly liberating in asking a bus conductor for "a ticket to Paradise." Moreover, I met conductors quite capable of coming back with, "That's the 109, mate, but I can get you to the Slough of Despond." I was acting at last. I might be stammering still, but in the astounding comedy there was a healing light. (Or was it just the false light smugglers used to lure cargo boats on the rocks?) After all, I can speak now—yet I hear the absurd in every earnest remark.

I told Margaret, "I love you," and she said, "Of course you do."

I don't know how they do speech therapy today. Perhaps there are delicate drugs that chill the proper lobe in the brain, or laser jets that can erase constriction. Perhaps it is still the same, a matter of finding your way out of the maze and raising merry riot in the street markets of the land.

I think I went to speech-therapy class every week for four years. In that time I grew older, of course, passing through periods that are often seen as troublesome and formative even in kids who have kissed the Blarney stone. Later on, we had specific psychotherapy classes. We were asked about our family life. I tried to explain my situation.

"Does that make you angry, sad?"

What a superb question. By then I was doing English at A level and having very good teachers ask questions about the meaning of poetry and drama, but I don't think I'd ever had so pointed and discerning a question about a feeling before. "Does that make you angry or sad?"

"Both," I said greedily.

"You'll be all right," said the therapist. "Try to tell the story."

It changed gradually. Kids at school said they saw no difference, except that I was talking more. And they were a little older and kinder, so they waited for me. With a good friend, Tony Hepburn, I wrote a paper for the History Society on the history of jazz. He read both parts to get it in during the lunch hour. But I could answer questions afterward.*

History had happened. For my fifth year at Dulwich I was in the History Remove and suddenly I had great

---

*By chance, after well over forty years, I got back in touch with Tony. He was coming to San Francisco. Would I join a historians' panel that he was mounting for a conference? We met. We were friends again. He read this manuscript and made some good corrections. A few months later he was dead.

teachers: Ernie Williams, the head of history; David Henschel, the most arousing speaker I had encountered; Reg
Colman, a steady guide to Tudor iniquities; and Jack
Gwillim, who had a wintry wit and shyness no matter that
he had been captain of one of the greatest Welsh rugby
sides of all time. Suddenly Dulwich was what it had promised. I was playing rugby and cricket. I was loving the
schoolwork. And I felt that maybe I could handle it all. At
which point I think I realized that I had got into the dark
hole from which I reckoned there was no escape. Growing
up and being normal. The implication of what talk means
in terms of emotional candor was daunting. And as I
talked more I felt my Dad sink into rage or middle age. I
cannot say that feeling was without revenge.

In Mitcham, Bert began to fade. It seemed his cancer
had returned. I had the idea of taking some of my records
and a record player over there. He and Grandma didn't
have a record player. I had some classical records and we
listened to them together and talked a little, though it was
still hard to hear what he wanted to say.

I was not sure what he wanted, to live longer, to last
longer, or just to be done with it. I did not know how to
talk to him about his life: how had it gone, was he disappointed or happy? In every way I could see, he seemed to
have led a humble life. He was a clerk. He had married and
had two daughters. He liked to see the horses racing on the
downs. He enjoyed a winning bet and was stoical about
losses. There was a grace about him, a way of showing his
reactions to winning and losing, a timing that let other
people in on the game. When I played records for him he
smiled with approval, as if he had always wanted to end

like that. And once or twice, sinking in deeper than the occasion, I heard the music myself—for the first time in my life. I looked up and he was smiling.

One afternoon in summer he died, in the garden. I cycled over. Grandma had put a white cloth over his head where he was still sitting, surrounded by growing flowers. The funeral home was coming. Alone with him, I lifted the cloth. He had the same peaceful expression I loved. But the struggle had gone, the tension. He seemed younger and more handsome, and I realized how far the last smiles had been his way of deflecting pain.

I told Grandma what I thought and she said, "I think you're right. Lord, he was a rascal, though."

"Was he?"

"You can't imagine!"

But I could. I took his rich inner life for granted, and I felt some rhyming when he died just a week before William Faulkner. That was neither here nor there, except that they were the two men who meant the most to me at that time. And Bert left me his books, a couple of hundred titles— George du Maurier, Somerset Maugham, *The Rubaiyat of Omar Khayyam*—and I folded them in with my own books, the Faulkner, *The Film and the Public*, Leonard Feather's *Encyclopedia of Jazz*, and the first biography of James Dean, by William Bast.

24

JAMES DEAN WAS DEAD before I saw him. In England, for reasons I have never understood and cannot endure, many American movies come out months after their American opening. Dean died—on the road near Paso Robles—on September 30, 1955 (even with a fading memory I do not need to look that up). And I daresay it was in the autumn of 1955 at least before I saw *Rebel Without a Cause* at the Granada, Tooting.

Something odd happened: there was a crowd at the theater, I suppose because of Dean's death, with a large part of it waiting in the deep-carpeted lobby, of the cinema that was the most decorated and extravagant in South London. So I decided to go in early before the end of the previous screening. This meant that I came into the dark just as Dean's character, Jim, edged into the planetarium in his attempt to save Plato (Sal Mineo). Suddenly, you read every bit of information you could get. And Jim seemed devious. He was trying to lure Plato out of the place, with police outside, and he borrowed Plato's gun for a moment and removed its bullets. That looked like a trick to get Plato; it seemed like cunning. And it was a clue to the way in which Dean was always—though not for long—artful, thoughtful, and not quite the vehemently sincere and spontaneous kid he claimed to be.

Now, I loved Dean, and when I at last saw *East of Eden*, his first film, I found one of the emotional focal points of my own youth. I did Dean, unashamedly, and I tried once to do him for Margaret so she would go with me to see *East of Eden*. She was Roman Catholic, yet she was already one of the best kissers I have ever met in a state of being (mine as much as hers) that really did not know how to go beyond the kiss yet. So to get her to *East of Eden*, I acted it out.

"Poor boy," she sighed. "He can't honor his parents."

"How can he?" I said. "His mother runs a whorehouse." Margaret shuddered. "And his father cannot express love."

"But you have to honor your parents," said Margaret. "God says so." How is it that such a person can kiss well?

I kidded her. It was my way of testing absurdity that was still kissing with something close to frenzy. And uttering such prim bromides. "But he is in another place," I said. "You have to see!" I knew she had to see Dean move to feel his mixture of shyness and mastery, and to possess it for herself, for us. But she didn't think her parents would want her to see the film, and she didn't feel able to exceed that lack of permission.

"Don't you trust me?" I said.

She looked at me. I've never known anyone more beautiful. "Should I?" she laughed.

"No, you should not," I said, and I felt myself sing away with the idea of becoming dangerous.

What I mean to say is that I saw from the outset that
Dean—in all his parts—was remarkable for knowing what
he was doing. That's what kids loved in him, and what
flattered them. He seemed to know more than his elders.
Famously, he and his secret, the Method, became known
for naturalness and raw feeling. But Dean is always saying,
"Look, a feeling. How do you like that?" And what acting
opened up to me was that feeling of hot and cold. There
are springs and streams in Yellowstone Park in which the
icy-cold water and water as hot as your best bath come on
you from different sides. I think it was scene making, or
story-telling, creeping up on me.

Some while later, I wrote the first thing I ever had published—an essay on James Dean—in the school magazine,
the *Alleynian*. Did the ghost of Edward Alleyn stir? Had an
actor ever been the subject in that magazine?

The magazine was just one of the bonuses at Dulwich if
you made it through to the sixth form. Once there you
were regarded as semi-adult and working toward university. The workload was hard and sixth-formers were
allowed to be antisocial, superior, sarcastic, and stuck up.
That encouraged our feeling of being a privileged club, an
endless debating society. It was notable and fascinating, I
thought, to see that the sour cream, having come through,
had picked up many of the styles and mannerisms of the
elite, but in a bantering, teasing way again. This is charac-
terisic of how many upper-class rigidities were relaxed by
exposure to lower-class ironies.

Last night I had dinner with an English couple who
have young children. All of us were the beneficiaries of private education, directly or indirectly. We talked about the

way I had had special access to Dulwich, what it did for me, and even for the school. You must understand that the experiment at Dulwich, the era of sour cream, is no more. It ended and has not been repeated, and I believe that it was closed down finally under a Labor Secretary for Education, Shirley Williams, in the late 1970s. So such schools are now fee-paying again, and "private" in the worst sense. Yet I want to say this as I observed it (and I was no fan of it at first): by the time I was in the sixth form, Dulwich was a very good school, at which old ideas and attitudes were engaged in a very useful struggle with sourer, more sarcastic, democratic urges. I regret that the "experiment" has been discontinued, and I marveled at the case made last night that the provocation by which lower-class children came in contact with their "betters" left them uneasy and awkward. I think I saw an opposite effect in the 1950s, in which the gentry had to quicken up to handle the "players," and in which the new social mix was lively and improving.

I do recall situations at Dulwich in which a pupil of old money let slip some degree of privilege—like having servants at home—and was greeted by hoots of derision from boys raised on household chores. That may have threatened a few, and may even have led to the termination of the "experiment." But I think it was all for the good. Further, I suspect that the kinds of radical and subversive energy that coursed through British society in the 1960s had something to do with the unforced interbreeding in schools.

It was in my time at Dulwich that the Gallery Club was formed. It was a sixth-former club and involved parties of boys going up to London to see a West End play. We had to have a teacher with us, but the club was run by the boys. I recall going up to town early one morning with cash to get a hundred seats in the gallery for *West Side Story*. It was the biggest event the club had ever had and a huge success. Ernie Williams, head of the history side, was our patron, and I recall him and his wife dancing at the end of that show. I hope the club functions still.

Somehow or other it proved beyond resources to start a Film Society. It was in the sixth form that some of us discovered the National Film Theater. This was the season, more or less, in which Ingmar Bergman was established as a cultural figure, with *The Seventh Seal* and *Wild Strawberries*. I heard from a friend at school, Paul Mayersberg, who went on to be a director and screenwriter of great merit *(The Man Who Fell to Earth, Croupier)* that a place called the NFT under Waterloo Bridge was doing a Bergman season; the Swede had been making pictures since 1946. So we went along. We joined the Theater. One evening we persuaded Mr. Henschel, one of our teachers, to join us—perhaps it was *Sawdust and Tinsel* or *Smiles of a Summer Night*—and to talk about it afterward.

My second piece in the *Alleynian* was on Bergman. My third was on Alfred Hitchcock, in the year of *Vertigo*. I was covering a private waterfront. That film was a failure when it opened in 1958, and very few could see into its cruel and desperate portrait of a director destroying an actress as he tried to make her into an ideal figure. I was possessed by the film, and by the very chilly beauty of its San Francisco. It was a film that took over my life in some ways, and by no means the largest of those was the chance that one day I came to live in San Francisco.

Margaret had dumped me. One evening as I moved to kiss her, she slipped a small gold cross out from under her shirt. I felt like Dracula being repulsed by one of his maidens, and she explained that she had promised herself to another boy, a fellow Roman Catholic. That was another club. Alas, I only fell in love with her all the more for being discarded. My most favored club has generally been kept for the unattainable. Is there anything more desirable than the thing you can't have? Is there a worse place to live for anyone who suffers from vertigo than San Francisco?

25

I MET ANOTHER GIRL, a lapsed Catholic, and we
escorted each other out of the darkest stages of sexual
ignorance without doing anything to diminish erotic
expectation. She was pretty, smart, brave, funny, sexy,
kind, as wary of gods as of parents. She was perfect, except
that she was number two. Put it another way, she was perfect except that she had met me, a person who had such a
chronic love of desire that I could hardly get my mind off
the lost or the forbidden. I'll call her Mary—though that
wasn't her name—because I trust that she's alive still somewhere and I wouldn't want her to be picked out for any
hurt.

While I was with Mary—and we went to the National
Film Theater together a lot—I would also go on prolonged
walks in that part of South London where Margaret lived,
on the chance of bumping into her. Was I aware that this
was madness? Yes. But I had been forbidden to telephone
Margaret. Letters were not answered. And I had a faith in

coincidence, I suppose, or gambling. It occurred to me at the time that there was a book in it—*The Journal of a Mad Lover*—in which the walker digests every great Chinese proverb about searching for the lost one and becomes an old man who one day bumps into an old woman and cannot recognize her. The gap between literature and madness is often very small, and anyone with sense might have guessed that I wanted to write books more than I needed to live a life. Alas, not even the LCC seemed to have classes or therapy available yet for this condition. But I remember at school that I discovered Wordsworth's *Prelude* and was entranced by its idea of a youthful landscape rediscovered later in life—and by the process of walking.

Though I was obsessed with the remote chance of seeing Margaret, I did begin to notice that South London was changing. Traffic had taken over. The High Road was no longer a gathering of genteel shops, it was a way to the south coast. Coaches, cars, and motorcycles went straight through, headed for getaway fun. The small shops closed. Larger markets came in their place. The family houses in Streatham were being remodeled as families passed away. They became collections of flats or rooms. Roads like Thirlmere became parking lots. London was picking up speed and prosperity. The extraordinary changes of the 1960s were beginning to appear in the distance like ghostly horsemen. But were they coming to free us or to invade?

The country was becoming prosperous. Clothes were changing. Color arrived. And very gradually there was color on the streets as immigrants came to London. All those parts of the Empire with awful ownership names— the Gold Coast, Rhodesia, and so on—were becoming

their own countries. It wasn't easy. There had been a move-
ment called the Mau Mau in Kenya, with bodies hacked to
pieces, and there had been the collateral slaughter as
Britain shrugged off India. Too late? Too casually done?
How else were such things to be managed? It seemed to me
that Britain, in its slow, awkward way, was doing the right
thing and changing the world. Of course, in the 1950s,
hardly anyone mentioned Ireland. But old attitudes were
breaking down. Not too far ahead, Penguin would challenge the law by publishing *Lady Chatterley's Lover*. There
was a trial, and a prosecutor asked one witness whether he
thought it was a book he should let his servant read—
without guessing that the bloke had never had a servant in
his life. And kids were making trouble.

On Tooting Bec Common, among all the other gentle
entertainments there had been a small lake on which one
could hire rowboats or canoes. At night the yellow craft
were tethered together. But then one morning the word got
around that all those boats had been smashed and sunk.
"Vandals" was the word, and it went with "Goths" or
"barbarians." But some kids, a gang, had done the deed,
not for profit, but just to spoil others' pleasure. They were
called "teddy boys" sometimes because of the way they
dressed, and they were associated with the new rock
music. They were violent, maybe, and "lost." Hardly anyone pointed out that they were the remains, the others, in
an educational system that picked on them at the age of
eleven and said they were in, but a failure. I had got
through that broken window, but a lot of kids I knew had
been sent to bad secondary schools, and those children
knew it was the kiss of death. You can't do that without
making some of those kids your enemies.

Not far from where I lived—toward Croydon—there had been the case of Craig and Bentley, kids who went on a rampage. One night in 1952 they had been together robbing a small factory. The police had come, and Craig, egged on by Bentley, had shot a copper and killed him. Here was the unusual angle: Bentley was nineteen, and he had been hurt in a bomb explosion in the war. He was said to be a bit "simple." And Craig was sixteen. But Craig was the stronger influence. In the end, Craig was sent to juvenile prison (though not forever) and Bentley was hung. There was profound dismay at the case, not just because kids had done this and had a gun to kill a policeman, but because the law had seemed so unfair. Mr. Macmillan kept on saying we'd never had it so good, and at last the congealed side of rationing and war damage seemed to be pushing back. But if prosperity was destiny for old England, juvenile delinquency and "hopeless cases" were part of the residue.

Whereas any kid who had lived through our postwar years knew how much luck had to do with it. One night a policeman found me trying to light a fire in a ruined house just to see what would happen. He could have been nasty. He could have taken me in. I might have been out of Dulwich with "communication problems" stamped on my file. Instead, he very calmly took me through what I was doing and asked me whether I didn't think it was pretty silly. I agreed. He sent me home. (But if I had been black?)

Suppose a copper had called me over on one of my endless romantic walks.

"'Ere! You!"

"Me?"

"Yes. My lad, you've been walking up and down this street for hours."

"Oh."

"What are you up to, then?"

"Well . . ."

"Go on."

"The truth?"

"It had better be."

"Well, Officer, I'm walking the streets in search of a beautiful girl I love."

The policeman's look is stern, stiff, starchy. He coughs discreetly. Then he lowers his gaze. "You too?" he says, and suddenly the sad life of a beat copper falls into place. The police in Britain now are modern. They have their TV shows and their nervous breakdowns. They're motorized, and the British accept that a lot of them need to carry guns. But at one time there were coppers, local, unarmed, conservative, but enlightened. John Arlott was such a man once.

In 1957, I believe, for the England vs. West Indies series, the BBC introduced *Test Match Special*. It was a program of ball-by-ball radio commentary of Test matches. And it made John Arlott one of those heroes of my life then. *Test Match Special* meant that you could follow the detail, and it put a tremendous stress on radio. There was television coverage of matches by then. But radio was the classic. Cricket, as some will warn you, is a slow game, and it is vulnerable to boredom. Enter Arlott, ex-cop, poet, wine authority, and man of Hampshire.

He might say, live on the air, and I am makng this up, "And at twenty to three the rains return, and they feel good. The purpose in the match begins to subside. A freshness arises. The players know that this moment won't last too long, but playing in the rain is such fun—they are like children again. Ah, that's it. They've had enough. And they're running off now like middle-aged men afraid of falling on the slippery grass."

Maybe I exaggerate. Maybe Arlott was tipsy half the time. But he was as insinuating on radio as Dylan Thomas or Samuel Beckett. I know that he was making it up as he went along, but the rhythms were flawless, and cricket was being ennobled. There was a team of commentators and experts—Rex Alston was another—and the team was good. But the game seemed to have been created for John Arlott's meditations. I began to collect his books—there was *Days at the Cricket*, about the West Indies tour of 1950—and the sound of his voice is still part of me.

Of course, no good could come from all that walking. You can invent the twist in which the walker gets trapped. This is how it happened to me. I was with Mary, walking along the High Road one evening after dark, and I looked but didn't quite notice at first that Margaret was coming toward us. I hadn't seen her in a year by then. So she was older and lovelier. I made a hash of the introduction. And Margaret stood there looking at the two of us with this smile that surely any proper Catholic God—not to mention the nuns—would have stopped in its tracks. I'm afraid that too much was left naked on the street that night.

"I see," said Mary later as I put her on her bus home. And it was said with a pitch of gloom too kind to want to crush my wicked elation.

26

A S DULWICH CAME TO A CLIMAX, I said I
would like to apply for Oxford rather than Cambridge—but that was only because I had all my
life supported Oxford in the Boat Race. And I applied to
Brasenose College because I recalled that it had had a number of outstanding rugby players. None of this was
informed or rational, but Dulwich imposed the issue upon
one and I followed along meekly. In due course I went up
to Oxford for about a week and stayed there in college
rooms while I sat the entrance examination. The rooms
were mean and cold, I thought. The food was dire. But the
exams were interesting. I had interviews, too, with dons
in the history department. We discussed issues in history
in depth.

They asked me what other things I was interested in
and I said cinema and jazz, and drew a blank. "We don't
do those things," the professors told me, and they gave
every impression of hardly knowing what they were per-

sonally. Years later, I was up for a fellowship at the University of Hull. Philip Larkin was on the panel making the award. He asked the same question, and I said jazz again—but modern, knowing his archaic tastes. His lip curled and I knew it was curtains for me. Larkin picked a poet, Douglas Dunn, but I rubbed his superior nose in the storms of Charlie Parker. "Hmmm," he said.

Of course, I knew, in the broader sense, that Oxford was not out to cater to me, that it was one of the great European seats of learning, and that Oxford itself was a place that must harbor as many unofficial tastes and pursuits as Paris if you had the time to search. But I was troubled. I did not feel certain that I was cut out for three more years—and, presumably, three intense years—of the kind of study I had done at Dulwich. I enjoyed history, and in studying Namier and Plumb I had got a first sense of Britain as a living organism, and as a place where reading and fiction came along like middle-class hobbies that might replace hunting and building great houses. But to know more about that subject was surely trapping oneself in a life of teaching. And I wanted to do something more creative, or less ruled by club and system.

Whenever such questions came close to being raised at Dulwich in the preparation for university, we were told that there were years awaiting us that would be the basis for our lives and careers. What have we been doing now? I wondered. And how were these tough years at Dulwich mere preamble? That didn't exactly fit with what I had felt about the place. Dulwich had been an ordeal and a challenge that gave way to a short season of sunshine. I knew that Orson Welles was twenty-five when *Citizen Kane* opened, and I saw that there was no time to be wasted. Moreover, I knew that in its great Gothic outlines and centuries of tradition Oxford was likely to intimidate me in just the way Dulwich had done.

There was also the fact that a place at Oxford involved some costs that my family, my father, and I would have to decide whether to face or not. That or I would need to work. Oxford offered me a place. Dad asked what it would cost. This was a moment at which he had made a maneuver with Grandma's house just like the one with ours. When Bert died, Grandma was left poor. So Dad purchased the house from her at a cut rate. She could invest the money he gave her and live in the house rent free. Mum was shocked at what he had done. She thought it was a cruel trick, and that Grandma had been deceived. But no one had the power to intervene.

So it was in that situation that one day I opened *Sight & Sound*, the magazine that came with being a member of the National Film Theater. Inside, I found a full-page ad for the London School of Film Technique. It offered a basic course of six months, "a comprehensive course in professional film making," it said. The curriculum was printed in the ad and covered the theory and history of film; an introduction to camera, sound, and editing; and ample opportunities for practical work. The school facilities included "two studios, editing room, cinema, projection room, dark room, lecture theater and workshop." It was located on Electric Avenue in Brixton, only a few miles from where I lived.

In 1959, this was the only site of any film education in Britain (apart from the BBC, where in television there was a trainee course). Not one university or college in Britain offered any education in film, whether criticism, history, or filmmaking. I had by that time accumulated notebooks that included about two hundred handwritten reviews of films I had seen. It seemed to me—with Mum's encouragement—the only sensible thing to do with the desire and energy I had for film. My model for those reviews, I suppose, were the pieces by Dilys Powell that appeared in the *Sunday Times*. She was another voice on the radio program *The Critics*, and I liked her voice and often shared her views, though even then I think I saw more virtues in American film than was common in those days.

I began to think of what might even be a choice, though I hardly dared mention it to anyone else except Mum—and she was in favor of Oxford. She said if I still wanted to I could do the film school later. At that time, her job was as secretary at a firm of accountants, and one of the partners at the firm was David Lean's father. She asked the father what he thought, and in due course a letter came to me from Lean. It was an enormous kindness and later made me feel guilty over not liking his final films. It was a careful letter in that it encouraged me but told me to be sensible. An Oxford degree would permit so many other things. Anyway, good luck.

A little research revealed that Lean himself had missed university, that he had started as a clapper boy at sixteen and had studied every craft of film as best he could—most notably editing—on the job itself. And he was married six times.

I went to look at the school on Electric Avenue. Upstairs in the school I met young people who taught there and I liked them. I saw the premises and guessed even then that the advertisement was on the generous side. But there were students all over the place and they were making films. It would be one hundred pounds for the basic course. I was given to understand that with my school record if I cared to apply there was a good chance I would be admitted.

They would have enrolled Puss in Boots if he had had a hundred quid.

Mum said I should talk to my teachers at Dulwich. Ernie Williams was genuinely shocked, as if all the work and care he had put in might be for nothing. "I believe you may be making a grave mistake," he said, and I did not doubt him. The school was horrified: its identity and plan were being questioned. Going to Oxbridge was the one way "class problems" could be finessed. But we got into talks such as we had never had before about life and I think he was impressed by my own feeling that I'd found something that was probably a mistake, et cetera, but right for me. He hadn't realized how many films I saw or the way I wrote about them. David Henschel was more neutral. He said he guessed I knew my own mind, and there was no earthly need or reason to do as you were told beyond a certain age. It was just that he had never found out the age!

Then Dad came to me, from out of nowhere. He didn't want to know what I felt about the choices. He didn't seek to know who I was. But he made this offer: he'd pay the £100 for the film school if in return I expected and sought nothing else from him in the way of later costs at university. If I changed my mind, it would be up to me. Vaguely aware that this objective observer was the owner of three houses—for there must be a house somewhere that he lived in most of his days—I felt the offer was, characteristically, to his advantage. In the long term, he was true to his word, for he left me nothing in his will.

I determined then and there that I was going to need to concentrate. If it was going to be film, then film it was. I decided to stop playing cricket. Within a week or two, the batting pads that Dad had given me and the very good bag for holding my equipment vanished. They were all gifts, but he reclaimed them. I don't know what became of them, but I was startled by the cold-bloodedness of it all.

The Dulwich establishment was grave and concerned. Ernie Williams never gave up trying to dissuade me. He was eager to have me believe that Oxford would be a great window on the world, and that academia was the threshold for everything I cared about. But then I found a book (a slender Penguin) called *Picture*, by Lillian Ross. It was an account of the making of a film called *The Red Badge of Courage* by John Huston. It was not a film I liked very much, but the report of how the men on the production thought and maneuvered during the job was fascinating and seemed to suggest a kind of everyday acting in show business that I relished. There was a man in the story, Louis B. Mayer, who was the villain of the piece. But he lived the way he talked and he indicated a lurid fairy-tale kingdom in Los Angeles where people existed in the limelight and their own blood and thunder without aging. If I had known then that the daughter and grandsons of Mr. Mayer would one day be my very good friends, I'm sure it would have encouraged my faith.

Something else happened. In my last year at Dulwich I had been made a prefect. Those were the most senior and privileged boys. We kept order most of the time. We were allowed to leave our jackets undone! And prefects could administer punishment. Well, the prefects had their own room, where justice was done. In my last term at Dulwich this happened. It seemed to me hideous but it helped me make up my mind.

The captain of the school—never mind his name—was holding court. A boy was up on repeated charges of cheeking prefects. He hadn't stolen anything or deflowered a younger boy—and such things did happen. He hadn't got drunk and damaged school property. At a school where wit and language were valued, he had said something funny and offensive to a few prefects. This boy—never mind his name—was someone I had known off and on. We had been in the same form a couple of years. We were the same age. We caught each other's eye in the crowded room.

His guilt was not in question in the mind of his judge, the captain of the school, who then administered what used to be called "three of the best"—strokes of a cane on the upturned bottom, though "strokes" is the wrong word. Nor should you believe in the establishment's own definition of "the best." Those three blows damaged me, no matter what they did to the victim. I doubt that much worthwhile in the school code was protected. I don't know how the "boy"—a young man—took the pain and humiliation in front of the assembled prefects. I daresay it was a kind of retaliation to class hostility: I suspect that the captain of the school paid fees and thought the miscreant was on a scholarship. But even if that was not the case, I didn't need the tradition that was being upheld.

About ten years later, Lindsay Anderson made a film called *If* . . . I don't know how good a film it is, but it's set at a public school and it has a rogue kid (Malcolm McDowell) who with a few fellows and his girlfriend starts an insurrection at the school. I know the feeling.

2 7

S O I WENT TO Electric Avenue. It was like putting my life in an open socket. I had meant to end this book here, with me at eighteen going on nineteen, with all the shock and burden of a large personal decision, a gamble. Or even a mistake? The film school was not what it advertised itself as, but that didn't get in the way of a massive amount of education, far more than I could organize at first.

But there was a night on Streatham High Road when I had just got out of a film. Old habits die hard, so I walked a little, and I was going down toward St. Leonard's Church when she stepped off a bus stopped at the lights. Just dropped off its platform the way everyone did. And I wasn't even thinking about her, yet there she was. That's a lot of patience to learn. I walked into the place where she had stopped still, smiling, but with a kind of anxiety on her face. As if maybe she had waited, too.

"Hallo," she said. "I thought it was you." She looked around. "Are you with that girl? She your girl friend?"

"How are you?" I said. In screen-writing class, I'd had a good lesson that day: answer a question with a question.

"Oh, all right, you know," she said—that awful London lament, "all right," or likely gone in a twinkling.

"I was looking for you," I said.

Her eyebrows went up and she was fifteen again. "You were? Why?"

"I don't mean tonight. For years."

"On the High Road?"

"Yeah."

I could see in her face something disturbed or alarmed by my gravity. After all, she was here, talking. Not vanishing. I was terrified of frightening her. Then she remembered. "We were supposed to see a film, weren't we?"

"Do you remember what it was?" I asked her. I had waited outside the theater over an hour.

"It was *Guys and Dolls*," she said. "You see, I do remember."

"You didn't remember to come."

She looked at me—Margaret, are you grieving?—with a smoke of amusement and sadness in her eyes and I felt she might know more about luck than I did. Are you angry or are you sad? Some of us need both.

"Well," she said. "I have something to do."

"Let me wait for you."

"I don't know how long I'll be."

"I don't mind."

She was thinking about it, so I told her, "I'm not going to let you go again."

"All right," she said, and now it was. She took my hand and we crossed the road. "I have to go to the church," she told me. There was a Roman Catholic church next to St.

Leonard's. There always had been. Her hand felt cold crossing the street and I was not sure what that indicated. So I squeezed her hand and she told me, "Don't worry."

"Are you coming in?" she asked, when we got to the church door. I hesitated. "It won't bite you." And then she said it again, "I won't let it bite you." So I went in and sat on a chair in the porch while she went deeper into the church for whatever it was she had to do. I could smell the incense and I could see through the gap between black velvet curtains that there was a light on near the altar. Like a night-light. I wondered if she would ever come back. But then there was a swish and there she was, carrying her coat. The material of her dress shone in the pale light and I could see the outline of her body.

"Can I kiss you in a church?"

"Best place," she said. And she leaned her neck back so that I could kiss her. Her lips met mine but did not quite join. She was watching me all the time. "My love," she said, and then her hands were up on the sides of my head and it was a kiss to cover all the years of walking. I felt her heart beating, and I wondered if she was unwell.

"Are you all right?" I asked her.

"Very," she said. "What are we going to do?" She had a way of asking a question so that it could have turned on the next minute or two, or the rest of our lives. I searched her eyes for a close reading, but then the smile came in that took a nearly carnal pleasure in my young frown. "I'm supposed to get home," she said, vaguely.

"Come and have a coffee," I said.

"Coffee!"

"I'll buy you dinner, then."

"I've had dinner. I should get a bus home."

"No."

"No?"

"Stay with me," I said. "I'll walk you home."

"You walk everywhere?"

"I like walking. And talking."

"Let's do that, then."

I helped her on with her coat (it was so heavy, she was so lithe). And we went out onto the street again.

"Why didn't you come to *Guys and Dolls*?"

"Oh, that was long ago. My mother told me I couldn't."

"Because I wasn't a Catholic?"

"She never said that. Because you were so serious. You still are."

"You don't like that?"

"It frightens me."

"You have another boy friend?" I demanded.

She looked at me askance and grinned. "Sometimes."

"Now?"

"You see, you are too serious."

"Now?"

"Not this minute."

"You're wrong," I said.

"I am?" Always that smile, taunting and leading me on.

"You've got me now."

"Oh, yes," she smiled, as if I'd just appeared. "You. Well, that settles that, doesn't it?"

"Are you going to university?"

"I don't know. Perhaps. What are you doing?"

"I go to the London School of Film Technique. It's in Brixton. Just started."

"A school to learn film? That's funny."

"Why?"

"You don't need to learn that."

"You do!"

"Well, you don't need to learn how to watch them."

"That too! I tell you what. I'll take you to the school."

"Now?"

"We can get a bus to Brixton—just a few minutes."

"It's nine o'clock already."

"It's early."

So we caught a bus and we sat upstairs in the front seat as the bus went down Brixton Hill, past the street that led to the prison. "I shot my first film there," I told her. "About a man coming out of prison."

"Who was the man?"

"An American at the school."

She grinned. "Would you put me in a film?"

"Would you take your clothes off?"

"Oh, shut up!" She broke into laughter. "All of them?" I shrugged and grinned, the spirit of compromise. "You could take a shoe off," I said, "so long as it's a high heel."

"I've got high heels," she said. "I wear them at my job."

"What's that?"

"A typist," she said, and she felt drab in the admission.

"A typist! That is absolutely insane, apart from being ridiculous that you are just a typist!"

She blushed. "You don't even know me," she said.

"What did you say?" Right there on top of a bus, a 159, I stared her full in the face and challenged her again to even consider that I didn't know her. "Don't ever say that," I said.

"I won't if you kiss me," she said. "You haven't kissed me for ages."

"If you'll promise not to be a typist I will," I said.

She giggled. But she was nearly limp with the thought of desire and transformation. She seemed to be watching her own movie, herself on a screen. "All right," she sighed, and buried her face in mine. There on top of a 159, and for so long that we missed our stop.

Crossing the road to enter Electric Avenue, she hugged my arm and said, "I'm always told never get off the bus in Brixton."

This was the Brixton where Oswald Mosley himself had been seen in the last year at a nighttime meeting, with floodlights and a gang of Blackshirts who might easily have been the wrestlers who trained in Brixton on an off night. There were West Indians new to the area, more every year, and in the market on Electric Avenue you could get plantains, mangoes, and fruits you couldn't name. These fellows were cheerful enough in the daytime, making their way in the busy streets among the insults. But there was natural anger on all sides, and the old Brixton, an underworld haunt that linked up with the notorious Borough High Street, where the cops used to go only in pairs and then never at all, had a political edge now, as Britain suddenly had to come to terms with the idea of shared citizenship. So there was bother about, teddy boys with knives and bicycle chains, and a general air of menace; any girl could have been told to stay on the bus as it dragged through Brixton. The big hill that led to Streatham was the measure of fresher air and greater security.

I knew the school would be open. Some people liked the editing room because it was largely empty, and in the studio one could play with the lights all night long. Students—in their way of working and in their enthusiasm for movies—were often those there late at night. So I did my best to act as if I was at home there. I had guessed the theater would be empty. And the precious 16mm print we had been seeing was still in its can.

"You ever seen *Citizen Kane*?" I asked her.

"What's that?" she said.

"There you are," I said, as if addressing the inner voice of history. "They haven't heard of *Citizen Kane*. Greatest film ever made."

"Who's in it?"

"Orson Welles, who also made it and inspired it and was only a few years older than us at the time."

"Will I like it?" she asked. Her smile curled up the corners of her mouth. She had cottoned on that her only chance was to tease him rotten.

"If you give it a chance, you will."

"You going to tell me what to look for?"

"Not a thing," I assured her.

She put on a demure face. "Can I sit next to you and cuddle?"

This was a predicament and a test of a critic who felt as I did for her. All at once I felt shy: I wasn't quite sure that she hadn't been ready to be taken to some alley and propped up against the wall in some *Gone With the Wind* of necking. But I wanted to impress her and guide her. She saw my face fall into impossible arguments, and she wanted the fire back.

"It's all right, I'll watch it if I can hold your hand."

I studied her, sitting in the tiny theater. She was more beautiful than she had been in my dreams for three or four years. "I love you," I said.

"Yeah, I know," she whispered, and almost helplessly, chronically, she reached out for me. "Keep kissing me, won't you?" she said. "I love it." I kissed her and I noticed that her breath had gone as flat as her voice could be. But then she breathed in and it was honeyed again, and her tongue was wrapped around mine.

"Is it really a good film?" she whispered.

"I love it."

"I thought you loved me."

"I do, I do."

The screening of the great work nearly didn't occur, for the simple reason that the inspired lover could not thread the projector properly. Was he anyone for a girl to have faith in? So I went away for a moment to the editing room: a tall, gaunt Irishman was working there; he came in in the evenings after his day job on a documentary about James Joyce's Dublin.

"Whatisit?" he hissed.

"I wonder," I said, "could you load a 16mm projector for me?"

"You can't do it?" he asked in disbelief.

"I have a friend who wants to see *Kane*."

"Is she as pretty as she looks?" he asked.

"You saw her?"

"A glimpse."

So, grudging and grumbling—which I would learn was his essential way (we would be best friends later)—Hickey left his masterpiece, nodded with drastic curtness to Margaret and froze her smile, and threaded the first reel of *Citizen Kane* into the Bell & Howell. "Are you ready?" he snapped at the two of us. I hurried to sit next to her. And then the lights went off and the middle of the night breathed off the screen.

"It's weird," Margaret crooned in my ear. "Where are the credits?"

"Just watch," I said, shifting a touch so that her arm could creep round me. Then that crested mouth was saying "Rosebud" to us.

"What did he say?" asked Margaret.

"Rosebud," I told her.

"What kind of thing is that to say?"

"It's his last word."

"Rosebud is a dying word?"

"Have you ever seen anyone die?"

"This is a strange way to start a film, by dying," she said.

Well, we or they (do you see them there, together?)—probably tried our best at thirty minutes of that great movie (in a quite respectable print) before the undeniable allure of the life force took charge. I had been at times attentive, eager, and excited—the great rush of the newsreel set her going even if she complained that it was too quick for a newsreel. And she had made it to the little house on the prairie, the haunting moment when Agnes Moorehead lifts up the window, calls, "Charles!" and you hear the wind moaning in the distance. She had seen the sledge and the lovely, mortal way in which snow made first one pile and then another on it, and what does that image tell us about time and memory? She had seen the camera move from the face of the boy to the strange forbidding but iconic image of the mother.

And it was then that she placed her two hands firmly on the sides of my head, like a mother packing a child off to bed, and drew me away and out of the film and away from Orson Welles and into her own compelling moment. Once and for all.

"I won't bite you," she murmured. But I didn't have to believe that.

On the bus later, going up the hill, she asked me, "So what is Rosebud?"

"It's the name on the sledge."

"What sledge?"

"When the man takes the boy away, the boy hits him with the sledge. And then we see it with the snow piling up on it."

"Oh, yes."

"Then at the end of the film, when no one has found out what Rosebud means, all of Kane's possessions are left, and the men move in to burn them in the furnace. One man picks up the sledge and the camera goes into the furnace with it, and just for a few seconds as it burns we see the word 'Rosebud.' And only we see it."

"We?"

"The audience."

Margaret smiled and said, "That's as it should be. We're the only ones who heard it."

"What do you mean?"

"At the beginning." She was figuring it out. "He says 'Rosebud,' and he dies?"

"Yes."

"Well, you see the nurse come into the room then, through the broken glass ball. She can't have heard the word."

I said, "It was just us there. You *were* watching."

"What do you think I am?" she asked.

"Don't you know by now?" I told her.

"So what does 'Rosebud' mean?" she asked.

"His childhood, I suppose."

"His mother sending him away?"

"That, and just the loss of his life."

"Do you think everyone's life is like that?"

"It's ours to lose. Or find."

"What about God?" she wanted to know.

I felt myself on the brink. "I can't believe in that," I said.

"Nor me," she said, and there was a bereftness, a loss of pity that broke my heart. "I get off here."

"You don't have to."

"Of course I do."

"I'm walking you home."

"Not all the way, please."

"All right." It was our contract for getting off the bus together. The streets were empty now. It was midnight. She walked as slowly as she could.

"It was a lovely night," she said. "Thank you."

"Tomorrow?"

"I don't know."

"Why not?"

"Look, I didn't know I was going to bump into you, did I?"

"I'll call you, then," I said. "It's not your mother still, is it?"

"It's nothing."

"I have to see you."

She nodded. "I'll give you a number. It's where I work. You can call me there." I wrote it down, and she said, "Yes, that's right, I love you, Mr. Kane." And we kissed just once more before Margaret darted away, calling out over her shoulder, "Don't get lost!"

CODA

THE STORY ENDS THERE? Well, no, of course not. Stories continue at least for as long as the leading characters live, and sometimes they go on much longer than that. But stories leave things out and introduce a shape, or an order, that no one noticed at the time or the moment. And if this book, so far, ends with a large decision, still the larger quandary that prompts it is left unsettled. So I must admit that I recognize that you might feel you need and deserve more. I feel the same about myself.

There's one thing I suspected was slipping away as I was writing the book. And when I read it over again as a whole, I knew my fear was correct. My mum is not quite there, not like she was in life. And in a way, that is the final mark of Dad's influence. That he left us was a gesture that claimed our story as being lived in his shadow. So the shape of the story as it ended makes him seem strong, whereas my mother was far stronger.

Mum was not dramatic. She did not tell stories or dominate routine. But she was the heart of our order and sensibility. Hers was the face that the movie kept cutting away to for eighteen or nineteen years, to see how the soul reacted and measured what was happening. And just because she accepted a lot that she might not like—like my father, more or less—does not mean that you ever doubted or missed her response. She was like Margaret that night; her face was always there—smiling, expectant, teasing, ravishing—so the movie moved along. A lover can do that for twenty-four days or minutes, maybe. But doing it longer requires a strength and a calm out of the ordinary— and a trust that the rest of us will keep watching.

Once he left her, she could have insisted on that fact. She said people like her didn't get divorced in the 1940s. But as you might guess, the war gave a great boost to that formalization of escape. She might have told our small world that Dad was a liar and a cheat (the things he had hated in his brother), and I'm not sure what that would have done to him. Was she giving him another chance? Maybe, at first, but not for long. Was she taking the "easy" way out? I think some believed that, but in fact I think the situation with my father made her life increasingly difficult. If she had gone off on her own, with me, I daresay some other man would have "rescued" her. There were other men over the years, and it was all very discreet. But if she had given a sign of courage, or recklessness, I think she would have been settled again in a few years. But that risk frightened her.

Still, I don't think she anticipated or even noticed at first the strange pressure it put on my father, to remember and observe all the petty deceits until he reached the point where he could do nothing but get up and leave the room when the questions became too threatening.

When I ask myself the key puzzles—why did my father leave us? why did he keep coming back?—one answer that deserves attention is that he could not escape the challenge, the hopeless challenge, of having to respond to her steady presence as calm and love. So he lost, when he was very competitive. Because she had love's access to the storyteller when maybe three sentences one day—three honest sentences—would have made him his dad's boy. This is what happened.

A few years after the events just described, I got married. (Not to Margaret, but you knew that.) You might have supposed that my father came home every other weekend for all those early years out of some sense of kindness to me, to be a father, to be there, to take me to sports, to observe the formalities. And I hope I've made clear how real that company was and how much I gained from it. But by the time I was eighteen our relationship had easily outlived his "selflessness." He was fifty-two, fit, lively. He could have fashioned a new life. He could have said to me, Well, I failed, but I did my best, and I'm sorry we're at odds now. Maybe later.

And in 1960, at that point, as I know now, there was a woman who lived with him on the other side of London—not a quiet or patient woman—who must have been turning to fury or poison that she was without him every other weekend, as well as every Christmas, Easter, Whitsun and Bank Holiday. Surely when she knew that I was gone she must have said, "Now—live with me. With us!"

He didn't. His schedule did not alter. You could argue that if everything came into the open, and if my mother chose finally to sue him for divorce and desertion, she would very likely have ended up with 10 Thirlmere Road (or a large part of its sale proceeds) as her due. And he hated to lose property, like any good Monopoly player. But he hated admission more. Maybe secrecy was his only hope—and that is close to madness.

A time came in the late 1960s when Dad played a key role in the negotiations by which the company he worked for was taken over by a larger company. He was a skilled businessman, and I'm sure he handled the plans very well. He was rewarded by being given early retirement by the new enterprise. This came as a great shock to him. (I don't think I ever saw him as emotionally surprised or unsteady.) And it erased his routine. He had no office to go to. He had no need for the other side of London. This was a moment at which he might have moved back to Streatham, the place where he kept his stamp collection—a telltale sign, some said. But if he had done that, then the other woman—let's call her Anne—might have gone to the courts as his common-law wife and got the house near St. Albans. So he kept coming home, using the car that had been part of his retirement deal.

In 1976, I was in America with my wife and three children. The marriage broke down (entirely because of my own behavior—so you have fair reason to wonder how deeply my father had affected me). My son and I came home from America on a boat, and while we were at sea my mother collapsed with a brain tumor. That was May 1976; she died early in September. The nursing process that went on that summer was interrupted by Dad coming home every other weekend and expecting to have his meals served to him. I remember making some of those dinners while the house was filled with Mum's repeated sighs, a helpless consequence of the tumor. He did not help either by caring for my mother or by making himself absent. It seemed as if he was coming home to serve his grotesque routine—and for nothing else.

My mother died, and Dad said he would be selling the house. In due course, he moved his stamp collection away. It was over twenty albums by then.

Not a word was said about his other life, or about the complex past. I sometimes tried to get him to talk, but still he would walk away and seek seclusion. Pushed closer and closer to intimate revelation, he steadily backed away. Of course, in private, he may have said his own "Rosebud." But in life we have to say it to someone. That is why the word is just a dead end in *Kane* and a terrible sign of that man's isolation.

In time, he informed me that he had married again—to Anne—and that he hoped I would visit them. Thus, at last, I met the other woman. By that time, her prettiness (and I have seen pictures) had turned hard and insecure. Why not? We did not get along, and I daresay it would have taken more than my dad's meager diplomatic skills for us to have had a better chance at a relationship. He handled things as if he had just met Anne, but of course in conversation things came out that showed they had been together for years. I later found a wartime identification card, dated 1945, in which she went by the name of "Anne Thomson."

He had an eightieth-birthday party, in 1988, attended

by me, my second wife, and his first American grandson, as well as his English grandchildren. I tried again to get him to talk about the past. He refused. He went away. He seemed in a rage at being asked.

In April 1993, he and Anne were involved in a mysterious car accident. I say "mysterious" because it was never quite resolved who was driving or how it happened. By June, he was dead, having never recovered from the effects of the accident. I visited him in the hospital shortly before his death. He was unconscious, though doctors were uncertain as to the cause of this. Some thought he was seeking to die, or waiting. I held his hand and talked to him about the past. And I felt then that a couple of times he squeezed my hand in assent. Or to show he could hear. But maybe that's how I wanted to remember it. If he had passed in complete, unaltered mystery, it would only have been in character.

Anne died in December 1994.

But is mystery character or the denial of it?

Is it over now? Well, the key players are dead, except for me. And I am left to tell the story, or to try to work it out. I realized long ago that I was probably doing what I do—worrying away at stories—because of the position I was put in by life. And when I finished this book, I showed it to my wife—my second wife—and she said she liked it and she thought it was accurate in terms of what she had seen and observed. But she said I had cheated a bit: I had written the book of a person who felt happy and lucky because of his life. Whereas, she said, quietly and kindly, I had been damaged by it all. And I know she's right, and I accept that in the telling I have neither explained it nor healed the damage. But when I am gone, and my childen, too, it will be a very small story as lived by a tribe of people who left little trace. But every one of us, for better or worse, is the center of our universe for a moment. And all we can do to signal our dumb longing to posterity is to leave a photograph and children or try to tell the story.

When the time came, I received a few photographs from my father's estate. They are not good pictures. I think he hated being "caught," whereas my mother loved the idea of the camera. You can see it in her gaze. When I look at the pictures of my father, though, I can see myself imprisoned there.

One other thing came with the pictures—a false mustache. It must have been something my father wore onstage once. I find it seductive and sinister—and the most personal thing of his I have.

A NOTE ABOUT THE AUTHOR

DAVID THOMSON has taught film studies at Dartmouth College, has served on the selection committee for the New York Film Festival, and has been the editor of the *Journal of Gastronomy*. He is a regular contributor to *The Guardian* and *The Independent, The New York Times, The Nation, Movieline, The New Republic,* and *Salon*. He was the screenwriter on the award-winning documentary *The Making of a Legend: Gone With the Wind*. His other books include *"Have You Seen . . . ?"; The New Biographical Dictionary of Film; Beneath Mulholland: Thoughts on Hollywood and Its Ghosts; Showman: The Life of David O. Selznick; Rosebud: The Story of Orson Welles;* and three works of fiction: *Suspects, Silver Light,* and *Warren Beatty and Desert Eyes*. Thomson lives in San Francisco with his family.

A NOTE ON THE TYPE

THE TEXT of this book was set in Sabon, a typeface designed by Jan Tschichold (1902–1974), the well-known German typographer. Based loosely on the original designs by Claude Garamond (c. 1480–1561), Sabon is unique in that it was explicitly designed for hot-metal composition on both the Monotype and Linotype machines as well as for filmsetting. Designed in 1966 in Frankfurt, Sabon was named for the famous Lyons punch cutter Jacques Sabon, who is thought to have brought some of Garamond's matrices to Frankfurt.

Composed by Textech, Brattleboro, Vermont
Printed and bound by R. R. Donnelley,
Harrisonburg, Virginia
Designed by Virginia Tan